Richard King is ⸻⸻ *How Soon Is Now?* (2012), w⸻ ⸻s Music Book of the Year. His writing has appeared in the *Observer*, the *Guardian*, *Vice* and many other publications. He is a regular contributor to *Caught by the River*. *Original Rockers* was shortlisted for the Gordon Burn Prize and longlisted for the Penderyn Music Prize.

Further praise for *Original Rockers*:

'An elegant panegyric . . . [with an] intoxicating sense of place.' *Guardian*

'⸻ghly personal memoir that vividly articulates the sheer ⸻ of musical discovery, the new or previously unheard ⸻ that attaches itself to a moment in your life, from ⸻ it becomes inseparable.' *Uncut*

'⸻ are a dozen different books packed into *Original ⸻rs* – a comic portrait of Revolver, a Bristol scene history and an analysis of British experimental music, for starters, but such abundance allows the book to imitate a ⸻ through the record racks.' *Q Magazine*

'⸻s celebratory, elegiac book, King remembers Bristol's ⸻er, an indie record shop that was idiosyncratic, eclectic and more than a tad intimidating to the casual browser.' *Express*

'Some of the finest music writing I have read in many a year. *Original Rockers* is a beautifully written and evocative re-making of one highly personal corner of the record shop decades – and one we'll all recognise.' *Test Pressing*

'*Original Rockers* is no misty eyed memoir, but rather a paean to the visceral thrills that music lovers and obsessive collectors will recognize immediately.' *Loud & Quiet*

'Wonderfully evocative music writing.' *Clash*

---

by the same author

HOW SOON IS NOW?

RICHARD KING

Original Rockers

FABER & FABER

To the memory of my mother,
Joan Hedda King

First published in 2015
by Faber and Faber Limited
Bloomsbury House
74–77 Great Russell Street
London WC1B 3DA

This paperback edition published in 2016

Typeset by Palindrome
Printed and bound by CPI Group (UK) Ltd, Croydon CR0 4YY

The right of Richard King to be identified as author
of this work has been asserted in accordance with Section 77
of the Copyright, Designs and Patents Act 1988

Modern Nature copyright © Derek Jarman, 1991; reproduced
by kind permission of the Estate of Derek Jarman and Peake Associates

Extract from 'Burnt Norton' as taken from Four Quartets
© T. S. Eliot with permission of Faber & Faber Ltd

A CIP record for this book
is available from the British Library

ISBN 978-0-571-31180-4

2 4 6 8 10 9 7 5 3 1

Some years ago I considered buying a stereo system. Much of my working life had been spent in record companies and I had also occasionally released music on small labels that had been started in order to promote artists that I considered unique, with little concern for commercial interest. I had consequently acquired a fairly large record collection that had also been expanded by forays into selling and trading vinyl. My records were played on fairly basic but adequate hi-fi that consisted of component parts from disparate, usually German or Japanese, manufacturers.

I was aware that various makes of amplifiers, turntables, pre-amps and power supplies had idiosyncratic characteristics and attributes and that in Britain stereo, built by what had often started as small family companies, was highly regarded. The discourse that surrounds hi-fi and the importance that is placed on such matters as the year of manufacture of a certain amp, or whether valves made of fragile glass were more responsive to a frequency than solid-state transistors, had discouraged me from researching further.

Similarly, I had also attempted to evade that rather strained obsession with the grading and provenance of vinyl on which many record collectors set so much store. I certainly struggled to see the necessity of such obsessions and was happy merely to own a release in reasonable condition on vinyl, as that was the format I had committed to during adolescence. Despite the unscrupulousness with which record companies had introduced the CD into the market, a market the format subsequently dominated for many years, I was always able to resist buying them. At my most supercilious I considered my refusal to contaminate my record collection with the unconvincing and digitally compressed binary audio of the compact disc a moral victory.

Although I was aware that my hi-fi system was workmanlike at best, terms such as 'pre-amp', 'power amp', 'power supply' and 'cut switch' continually struck me as having little to do with the pleasure of listening to music. I felt that they suggested a triumph of function over content that belonged to the type of person who prioritised the tactile aspects of buttons and the thickness of speaker cable over the beauty and wonder of recorded sound. For many years I had also felt weary of the overbearing preoccupation with technical detail and pristine condition that seemed to be obsessions mutually shared by record collectors and hi-fi enthusiasts.

Eventually I conceded that if I was prepared to gloat over owning several thousand records, another person was justified in pointing out that, by listening to my vinyl on battered, second-rate equipment, I had never truly heard it.

All too aware that my prejudices often hinder me, I began investing in a stereo system that would do justice to my acquisitions.

There was another reason for this purchase. As I spent time among my records I was drawn closer to their physical presence; on occasion I felt them looming on their shelves with a latent sense of purpose. I was at times almost able to imagine them watching over me, as if by having been held, inspected and played they were somehow rendered sentient. For the first time in my life I instigated a rather arbitrary filing system and arranged the records accordingly. I had previously allowed my records to organise themselves, mainly because I felt that taken as a random and unordered whole they became more than the sum of their parts. As I began the process of filing I was reminded of how much pleasure records gave as objects, and that holding a few albums or 12" singles under one's arm produced feelings of anticipation and excitement.

I was also once again becoming dextrous at handling vinyl. I could turn a record over and replace it on the deck in one fluid motion and was newly adept at perching an unsleeved record between my third finger and extended thumb in readiness to place it on the turntable. These actions and emotions brought me closer to an environment that I had once inhabited with an unconscious regularity as innate as breathing, but one that might now be lost to me: Revolver Records, a shop in Bristol.

During its lifetime, by the most straightforward definition, Revolver was an independent record shop, one with a reputation for stocking and specialising in iconoclastic and esoteric records rather than more quotidian Top 40 music. It had many other qualities. Its lack of shop front and its long approach corridor, one that was of sufficient length to feel somewhat intimidating, ensured Revolver had a particular atmosphere. The shop's institutional expertise lay in certain strands of music, such as reggae, dub, free jazz and psychedelia. As well as managing its reputation, Revolver curated and stocked an anti-canon, a permanent selection of records that it considered to be essential purchases, one that had been assuredly created through years of developing and then responding to its customers' tastes.

For these customers Revolver ceased to be merely a shop and became the locus of their musical consciousness.

The shop lacked any formal store front and was entered through an anonymous and peeling doorway which abutted the Triangle, a one-way thoroughfare at the junction of Park Street and Queen's Road, two of Bristol's most prestigious streets in the city's bath-stone-suburb, Clifton. Although the shop was at street level, the average passer-by was completely unaware of Revolver.

Anyone working in the shop was less interested in selling the weekly deliveries of new releases than in delving through the racks of rare and obscure records that were hidden in a back room away from the public's view. This dusty annexe to the shop's main activities contained a lifetime's worth of music that could only be absorbed by listening to one record at a time.

As an undergraduate I visited Revolver almost every day before I finally managed to secure a job there, for around three or so years, during the mid-1990s.

Once the door to Revolver was opened in the morning, the alarm had been turned off and the lights turned on, any other interpretation of everyday life was hard to imagine. Instead time was told by the length it took for a needle to reach the end of the run-out groove, or was dissipated altogether. Days would drift by and we would find ourselves still there behind the counter long into the night, unable to leave, the shop lights off, our listening illuminated by the blue lights of the stereo.

The reasons I had for wanting to dwell once again mentally and emotionally in Revolver were confused and varied. None of us is immune to nostalgia, particularly when the senses are at their most vulnerable. To hear a forgotten or rarely listened-to piece of music and be reminded of the person one once was is to be out of one's depth. The pleasure of listening to records during such moments is as brittle as the dark, hardened fibrosis that covers scar tissue, but by spending hours among my records once more, ordering them, cataloguing them, placing them in new plastic sleeves and above all by playing them, I felt as though I was in some abstract way inhabiting once more the shop's tatterdemalion atmosphere.

Certain body movements, such as the particular angle at which one crooks one's head to read the spine of an album, reminded me of being in Revolver. As I hooked my new turntable's tone arm out of its cradle on to my forefinger and let the stylus drop on to a record, I felt I had resumed a habit that might again become second nature and I realised that my memories of Revolver had undergone a process of reification.

The physical aspects of listening to a record, such as the sensation of a bass line reverberating in one's chest, or the barely discernible twitch of the fabric housed in the right angles of a speaker cabinet, felt as significant to my understanding and enjoyment of music as the history or biography of those who had created it. This was due entirely to Revolver, the dimensions of its rooms, the character of the people who had populated it and its location in their hearts.

We regard nature and the environment as though they are a constant source designed for our rehabilitation and amelioration. There is a sense that in the open air we are revived and becalmed. Revolver, an airless and enclosed space, had always seemed to me to be a phenomenon as singular and uncultivated as anything found in the natural world. In my recollection the shop was a landscape with its own customs, language and ritual. Now extinct, at least in the confluence of my memory and imagination the shop remained dormant and I felt an overwhelming desire to explore again its space. Although they lay deep in my subconscious, the routes back to Revolver revealed themselves with every record I placed on the turntable.

In terms of its contribution to music in Bristol, Revolver had a rich history. The shop had nurtured and informed many of the city's musicians, including those who had gone on to have recording careers. It also helped aspiring groups and artists release and distribute their own work. Revolver similarly provided an individual customer service to its regular clientele by locating and ordering hard-to-find releases from all points of the globe, but in my mind its greatest legacy was its resolute spirit and ardour. To purchase a record at its counter was to become involved in a limitless series of negotiations, diatribes, monologues and disputes, most of which, though by no means all, were held in an atmosphere of joy and high anticipation. These exchanges were held between a staff and customers who regarded the depth of their love of music as immeasurable and sacrosanct, to such an extent that the atmosphere in Revolver regularly felt hysterical.

The shop's ambience could at times feel hostile and intimidating, and as a high-street retailer, with the sense of universal access which that term implies, it was hardly faultless. I have heard of only three, possibly four, former female employees, although 'employee' or 'staff' suggests a formality and rigour in the shop's affairs that were never present. In around 1982 the Bristol listings magazine *Venue* ran a feature on Revolver that included a picture of those present behind the counter on the day their photographer had visited. As well as its then proprietors, Lloyd Harris and Mike Chadwick, there are two women in the photograph whom, despite several phone calls and conversations, I have been unable to identify. They are wearing the type of clothes and hairstyles one might associate with the culture wars of the era and have a confidence in their smiles that is beguiling.

Revolver was an environment often dominated by men, but it rarely tolerated the affectations and false modesty that allow pedestrian male identities to flourish. Light-hearted or superficial banter was vehemently discouraged; the shop was far too neurotic a place for such settled patterns of behaviour.

The mood of Revolver suggested a number of possible previous lives: the headquarters of a leading publication in the underground press, a backwoods stilling shed or the anteroom of a hastily assembled council chambers that had been prepared in readiness for the onset of the revolution. There were instances when the shop often felt like all of the above simultaneously, but the overpowering atmosphere was of a heady freedom prompted by the realisation that one was surrounded by thousands of records.

At the far end of the room was the shop counter, which stood at elbow height and seemed purpose-built for loitering. The counter could only be accessed from a side door in the corridor, which gave the staff, who sat or stood behind it, an air of absolute indifference. Behind the counter were piles of old magazines, rows of cassettes, abandoned displays of stylus cartridges and never-ending mounds of junk and paperwork. This debris reached to the furthest corners and recesses of the back room, but above all, there were innumerable rows of records.

Over time, as the conventions and mechanisms for remaining solvent in the music trade were routinely rejected, the shop felt increasingly as though it was a location for an unspecified form of resistance. Revolver lacked a credit- or debit-card facility and only accepted cash or cheques. It similarly declined to be included in the national chart-return system, thus rendering all of its sales ineligible for the Top 40, or any other chart for that matter. Of more significance was the fact that the lack of chart recognition ensured that on their arrival in the shop, the barcodes that record companies insisted on placing on their releases became impotent. If Revolver traded on its own precarious terms, then the music it bought and sold would do the same. In its refusal to embrace the structures and protocol of retail, Revolver began to resemble a front line, a border between the low commerce of selling records and the continuous shifts in the musical and psychological imagination.

To linger at the counter at Revolver was to occupy a dream state, where any particular album or song played on the shop's stereo sounded characteristic of this peculiar, virtually windowless place.

*

A scant hour or so survives of the footage filmed at various recording sessions at Lee 'Scratch' Perry's Black Ark Studio, located towards the rear of his property in Cardiff Crescent in Kingston, Jamaica.

During a sequence shot in 1977 for a documentary titled *Roots, Rock, Reggae*, Perry can be seen in the Black Ark's compact control booth directing a recording session. His demeanour is animated as he organises the musicians by shouting and gesturing through the window that overlooks the studio's live room.

Members of the Heptones and Junior Murvin are seen standing in front of rows of microphones as they run through the harmonies of a chorus together. This is edited with footage of the Black Ark house band, the Upsetters, playing around a melody line with a similar blend of high spirits and serenity. Perry appears fit, shaking his head and clapping, cutting the air in time to the song's rhythms and periodically punching and turning the controls of a Mu Tron Phasor. This rudimentary piece of equipment was used in counterpart with a Roland Space Echo tape delay to create the aural equivalent of dust that Perry appeared to fleck across every Black Ark recording. Two or three minutes into the film, when the producer is in mercurial flow and smiling as he shifts between the mixing desk, the control window and the phaser unit, the documentary's narrator starts describing his subject.

'Scratch's real name is Lee Perry,' he begins. 'He records all the greats, including Bob Marley. Even Paul McCartney is coming here from England because Scratch has a sound and a riddim of his own. He calls it "rockers". When Scratch begins a session, first he balances drum and bass for the basic rhythm. Ghetto music, always drum and bass.'

At the time the programme was made there were several contemporary producers and musicians in Jamaica who, if they had felt the inclination, might dispute the narrator's attribution of the word 'rockers' to Perry. It seems unlikely, however, as the derivation and usage of the reggae lexicon was of little consequence to those who played the music, particularly when considered in comparison to the numinous and physical effects it had on the listener and those involved in its creation. The drummers Leroy 'Horsemouth' Wallace and Sly Dunbar are usually credited with inventing the rockers rhythm in the Channel One Studio at Maxfield Avenue, an area of West Kingston more suited to the term 'ghetto music' than were Perry's premises in the upmarket suburb of Washington Gardens.

At Channel One, deep in the tenement yards, Horsemouth and Dunbar accentuated the first beat of every bar and introduced extra clap sounds and rim shots on the snare drum. On first hearing, these fills and snare taps could be mistaken for outboard effects such as delay or reverb added during the track's mixdown, but rather than interfering with the structural flow the extra emphases placed in every bar had the effect of sharpening and intensifying the rhythm.

To attempt an exact definition of the rockers rhythm is to misinterpret the reasons for its creation; the rhythm was less a specific drum pattern than an overall sense of motion. Rockers is often preceded by the adjective 'militant' as, together with the army fatigues worn by many reggae musicians in the 1970s, the rhythm suggested an intensely felt sense of impetus and purpose.

Whatever its interpretation, the rockers rhythm was the foundation of the roots music that formed the basis of reggae from around 1972 to 1978, a music and culture that expressed the realities of life for those suffering under the unforgiving sunlight and the political and social turmoil of Jamaica at the time.

On the B side of singles from the period, the lyrical messages of roots: the calls for unity, prayers for transcendence and rejection of the injustices of tenement life were replaced by the 'version'. The version was an instrumental dub that often featured mere fragments of the melody and vocal lines, and concentrated on creating a hollowed-out and abstract reinterpretation of the original. The residual space that had been left by stripping the song back to its bare rhythmic bones was overlaid with effects that magnified and amplified its dimensions. Suggestive half-heard tones and frequencies created by manipulating the instruments with echo and delay appeared in the track as though they had been introduced by an eerie and indeterminate logic. The sound of the version and the ghostly presence of dub within it was a sonic representation of 'Dread', the psychological manifestation of life's hardships given flight and devotional counselling by the power of the producer's imagination.

The phrase 'record producer' might be synonymous with a studio engineer who has an overinflated sense of their role in the making of an album, or of someone who considers their position within the recording industry to have a certain significance. At the mixing desks of Kingston the producer was simultaneously an auteur, a small businessman and an evangelist who harnessed a spiritual and creative energy by synthesising his technical dexterity with a conviction that could be mistaken for opportunism. Dub in particular was a music that required the producer to re-imagine the raw material of an instrumental backing track as a potential sacrament.

The dub album *Original Rockers* was a collection of singles released on the producer Augustus Pablo's Rockers International label in 1979. In accordance with the conventions of the island's music business, Pablo ran his label from a yard and distributed its output through the record shops of Jamaica. Once they became available to the public the recordings were left to fare in the indistinct and unquantifiable hinterland of the country's copyright laws. The singles compiled on *Original Rockers* had been recorded between 1972 and 1975, and about half the tracks had been created at Channel One; the seven-year period from the inception of the recordings to their eventual appearance as a compilation covers the pinnacle of roots music.

Roots, in a similar manner to rockers, passed beyond the idiomatic and became a word with no fixed definition, but one that was felt and understood by anyone who used it in conversation.

The origins of the word 'rockers' and the idiosyncrasies of its usage was a conversation that I heard unfold on several occasions over hours spent at the Revolver counter. The importance of a single's version to the evolution of dub was also explained to me in fine detail. These hours would be punctuated by a close listening of the records under discussion, a communal activity that was regularly followed by moments of detached quiet. The reflective, silent pauses felt as though they were a necessary procedure that had to be experienced before conversation could resume.

Throughout its existence Revolver sold tremendous quantities of dub and reggae records. Roots singles that were compiled into albums became a crucial element of the shop's canon, while during its heyday the shop sold as many formats of reggae that its supply and distribution chains could provide. For years long after its release *Original Rockers* was an album that would usually sell within days, if not hours, of being placed in the shop's racks. I can think of no other record so emblematic of the telepathy and familiarity that existed between Revolver and its customers.

Other conversations at the counter could be as heartfelt and comprehensive as those concerning the origin of rockers. In 1966, during the sessions for *Revolver*, a Leslie speaker housed in a Hammond organ was used as an effect to distort John Lennon's vocals for the song 'Tomorrow Never Knows'. The Leslie speaker had been designed with rotating components that modulated any signal sent through its drivers and as these moving Rotor parts were applied to a voice, the sound became submerged and supernatural. Within a few months of the album's release this studio trick was quickly emulated and the wavering Leslie speaker effect became a signifier of a particular strain of British psychedelia.

The shop often played fairly obscure late 1960s records, although it was difficult to hear or purchase them in the original. Songs such as 'My Clown' and 'Dandelion Seeds' by July or 'We Are the Moles' by the Moles, a record once falsely attributed to the Beatles in a psychedelic PR stunt, were only ever available as badly mastered CDs or on bootleg vinyl of uncertain origin and legality. These releases were placed in a rack near the counter that included compilations with such titles as *Electric Sugar Cube Flashbacks* featuring similarly obscure recordings by Family and Wimple Winch. The rack had been created specifically for this genre, one for which Revolver had invented a name: 'Town Crier Psych'. The debut Family single 'Scene Through the Eye of a Lens' included on *Sugar Cube Flashbacks* features every instrument processed through a Leslie speaker. The song's title would have been an equally appropriate name for this section of records. Whereas 'Tomorrow Never Knows' used the rotating Leslie speaker to simulate the uncontrollable rush experienced at the onset of an LSD trip, 'Scene Through the Eye of a Lens' adjusted its tempo to reproduce the minuscule distortions and refractions that embody its seemingly endless duration.

Many of the shop's customers had developed arcane tastes having spent lifetimes accruing information from fanzines, out of print music books considered to be hallowed texts, or from the sleeve notes of deleted compilations that had been written with fanaticism. Our clientele knew that by entering Revolver their visit ensured the shop was transformed from a liminal space into a threshold, a portal where the shop counter was not merely a location for purchases but a point of departure for the sharing of an obsessional love of music and a wonder at its ability to transfigure the everyday.

*

In time, over the course of several months, whenever I allowed my hand to wander across the shelves of my record collection I was making spiritual contact with Revolver. As I selected an album to listen to and positioned the vinyl on the deck I felt the slightest of quickenings in my heart. Once the record rotated on the turntable, its dark gloss circles caught the light and I gazed as it refracted its shafts into endlessly repeating curves. Transfixed by its circular motion I had to force myself to break my stare.

These instances of reverie became frequent. A tear along the seam of an album cover now held a historical significance. Handwriting on records, usually in biro and bearing the name of a previous owner that had never previously been noticed, had become a newly discovered set of instructions. I felt as if I was being directed back to Revolver, towards its dust-covered shelves, its muted carpets and walls, towards its lack of daylight and its insulation from the world outside, an insulation that had been provided by an eternal stock of vinyl.

Revolver never bought, sold or played music in any accepted sense. Rather, the shop and its customers experienced music as if they were practising rituals. I had renewed my familiarity with these rituals to a point where I was able to participate in a form of time travel, to a journey's end where the emotional effect of music was as overwhelming and illuminating as the moon at its nearest and fullest, as if revealing an eternal, solitary truth.

2

One morning I walked into the back room of Revolver and immediately tripped over a bicycle, my fall broken by a pile of discarded record boxes and cracked PVC covers. The bike was usually stored against a shelf of vinyl hidden in a recess. It belonged to Roger, Revolver's proprietor, who had moved the bike from its customary place in order to improvise a temporary signwriting studio. Around his feet were old coffee pots full of stubs of pastel-coloured and white chalk. In his hand was a blue J-cloth he had just dampened in the sink which he was now slowly running across the surface of a sturdy five-foot-high A-board.

In the breathless manner with which he had built the display boxes, counter and shelves and wired and fastened every fitting in the shop, Roger had constructed and painted the A-board with a confidence that combined childhood enthusiasm with dexterity. I had first encountered then befriended Roger, as one of the many customers whose primary reason for visiting the shop was to hold prolonged conversations at the counter. These exchanges began as slightly competitive discussions about obscure records before growing into a form of theatrical, absurdist exchange on which the shop's reputation thrived.

Roger was one of the most remarkable people I have ever met. His supple and well-built frame was evidence of his love of cycling and of moonlighting from the shop as a handyman and builder, an interest that ensured he spent regular periods of time away from Revolver, fitting roofs or hanging doors within the informal Bristol economy to which the shop, via the exchange of records for other miscellaneous goods and services, often contributed. Unlike many record-shop proprietors, Roger was in rude health and took care over his appearance. He had a thick head of dark silver-flecked hair that, along with his aura of briskness and his tendency to be boisterous and ready to engage anyone who visited the shop, meant his age was difficult to determine. I never established how old Roger was, but when I started working in the shop I assumed he was in his forties.

Roger had taken over Revolver from the shop's founders, who had left to concentrate on running a record distribution company of the same name. He had arrived in Bristol from Cheltenham, where he had known and played in a band with the musicians who became Pigbag. At times his manner could appear evangelical, almost crazed, to the point where customers felt intimidated and vowed never to return. His willingness to give his opinion about enquiries for records he considered second-rate occasionally had consequences. I once saw a visitor distribute the contents of a divider bin across the shop floor and shout, 'Take this lot to the tip then!' in response to Roger's assertion that the record the visitor was searching for was more likely to be found in a skip than in Revolver. A few months later a colleague informed me that such retaliations were not without precedent.

In a city as lackadaisical as Bristol, a natural extrovert such as Roger was occasionally considered volatile or opinionated; but his opinions were invariably worth hearing. His knowledge of every genre and style of music, especially jazz, was unparalleled and had begun at an early age. He told me stories of wandering into Marine Ices in Chalk Farm in need of sugar after nights spent in the Roundhouse as a stoned teenager; later he ran a record stall in Portobello Road where Brian Eno had been a regular customer, for albums by Fela Kuti in particular.

As Revolver had no store front Roger had made the A-board to help summon interest. It was positioned every morning alongside the shop's entrance where the careful design used in its decoration was at the mercy of Bristol's weather patterns. On the near side of the board was written that week's releases and details of any new stock and consignments that might be of interest to our customers. The reverse side was taken up with what had become known as the Revolver alphabet, an A to Z of bands and artists that represented the ethos and taste of the shop but whose releases, given our cash flow, were far from guaranteed to be in stock. The contents of this inventory were usually discussed by committee, one whose decisions were disregarded by whoever had decided to write up the board and who instead substituted the agreed list of names with one derived from their prejudices and imagination. A typical board might start with 'Ayers' and 'Buckley', which gave the impression of the morning register at a provincial boys school.

The alphabet gradually grew detached from such orthodoxies and began to bear the hallmarks of a more conceptual approach. Roger might create an imaginary band name or, as he occasionally did, satirise some of the shop's clientele. As a customer I had once walked passed the board and was compelled to stop and attempt to decipher a word placed in between 'Momus' for M and 'Ornette' for O (in keeping with its vernacular, jazz musicians were referred to by their first name). Along nearly the entire length of a line in the alphabet was written 'Neoohhhvarhhhniahhl'. Inside the shop I had waited for a quiet moment before asking Roger the meaning of this linguistic composition. 'Nirvana,' he replied, evidently surprised at my confusion. 'Spoken in a thick Bristolian accent.'

Although the names written on the board were notionally interchangeable, the repeated inclusion of a few artists was assured. This was no more so the case than with Can.

When I began working at the shop, Can were revered, but the band's music retained an air of mystery and secrecy, one that was shared among acolytes but had little resonance other than being an influence. In part this was due to the difficulty of finding their releases. Although the Can catalogue had been reissued on CD, the band had yet to receive any critical reassessment or undergo the careful remastering that accompanies canonical status. Instead their albums were available in rather piecemeal editions with thin facsimile sleeves that lacked the resonance of the originals.

The sound quality of the CDs was equally insubstantial, as if the sound engineer had digitally remastered a low-resolution cassette from a vinyl copy of each album rather than returning to the original master tapes.

The albums Can released in the 1970s had been housed in thick, cardboard gatefold sleeves with dramatic, gnostic artwork and which had long been prized by record collectors. Although I prided myself on enjoying older records far more than anything written about in the contemporary music press or in the charts, I was unfamiliar with Can's recordings. I had first heard their name as I witnessed Roger selling 'Fools Gold', a 12" by the Stone Roses, to an undergraduate. As he completed the transaction he debated with a regular customer to what extent the Stone Roses had committed larceny by plagiarising Can for their latest release and whether the German band might be in a position to sue.

'Straight rip-off,' said Roger, but, 'This lot . . .' he nodded towards the student who had just completed what was likely to be his final Revolver purchase, 'straight over their heads.'

In a corner behind the counter, hidden from sight, was piled a large assortment of bootleg CDs and other recordings whose provenance was never fully explained.

Two separate copies of live Can performances from their mid-decade eminence were included in this hoard of illicitly produced music. Their titles, as was common with bootlegs, demonstrated a fan's stoned fanaticism. The first CD was titled *Unopened*, in a rather laboured play on words on the official 1976 Can compilation, *Opener*. The second bootleg was named *Horror Trip in the Paperhouse* for the song 'Paperhouse' on *Tago Mago*, an album, one of several, that were frequently described in Revolver as 'the greatest record ever made'.

Towards the end of an uneventful day I loaded *Horror Trip in the Paperhouse* into the CD player. The recording was of a largely improvised free concert the band gave in the Sporthalle, Cologne, in 1972. An hour later I realised there had been no visitors to the shop and outside the light had grown dark. I had been oblivious to my surroundings for the duration of *Horror Trip in the Paperhouse*.

Until advances in digital recording, concert bootlegs were taped on to cassette either by a member of the audience via a microphone and recorder concealed within a coat pocket, or directly from the signal at the mixing board positioned in the middle of the concert hall. Once these recordings were duplicated, the sound quality depreciated and gained the subaqueous echoing quality that could be heard on *Horror Trip in the Paperhouse* and that suited the music of Can. The performance essentially consisted of a single, long jam that occasionally fell into a structure recognisable as one of their songs.

Can's bass player Holger Czukay had been a student of Stockhausen, as had the keyboard player Irmin Schmidt, and Jaki Liebezeit, the band's drummer, had once played in the Manfred Schoof quintet, one of West Germany's few and respected free-jazz ensembles. Czukay and Liebezeit synthesised the economy of James Brown's rhythm section with the theories and transcendental qualities of minimalism. On *Horror Trip in the Paperhouse* there was a devotional intensity to Can's music that was overwhelming and had consumed me as I sat listening in the empty shop.

In the back room of Revolver was a set of floor-to-ceiling shelves, each four feet in length and overfilled with records arranged in loose alphabetic order. The artist names corresponded with those written on the Revolver A-board. This hidden wall of vinyl was irreplaceable and kept from the public and discussed by the staff only in secretive murmurs.

I had looked along its shelves in vain to locate albums by Can that I presumed would be filed under the letter 'C' but had been perplexed by the lack of their records.

One evening I locked the front door at closing time

then scoured the length of each shelf, finely reading the millimetre-thick spines of every album. Eventually I located a complete set of Can records arranged in an inexact chronological order. The collection started with an original United Artists copy of their debut album *Monster Movie* when the band had been known as The Can and concluded with the eponymous record the band released in 1978 before commencing a decade-long hiatus. Rather than filed under 'C' for Can the records were located in the 'K' section, for Krautrock.

I began to play Can during slow periods in the shop. One afternoon I heard the customary sound of the back door shutting and the slow click-clack of his spokes coming to a halt that signified the arrival of Roger. However dispirited he might feel by the end of the day, from a disagreement with a customer or a distributor telephoning to demand payment of an invoice, Roger always turned the corner towards the counter smiling and sparkling, flushed from his cycle ride.

As he approached the stereo his face changed suddenly.

'Can't have Can on in the shop!' he exclaimed as the glow from his journey quickly subsided.

I was aware that Can were a band he revered with an atypical starriness and with whom he had started a relationship as a student in Swansea, where he had promoted a concert by the band at the university. I was confused by his reasoning and asked for clarification.

'I get too involved!' he replied, clearly agitated.

As Roger entered the stereo was playing 'Yoo Doo Right', the sixteen-minute song that takes up the entire side two of *Monster Movie*, he withdrew to the back room slowly shaking his head. I had never seen Roger in such a serious state and was uncertain whether he was angry. His head-shaking grew more extravagant and I slowly realised that what I had mistaken for a gesture of reproach was in fact the beginning of Roger's physical capitulation to the intractable groove of 'Yoo Doo Right'.

There is a passage during the song in which the drums and bass fall silent and only the voice of Malcolm Mooney and a single drumstick can be heard. Eventually the instruments resume and the guitarist Michael Karoli summons an overdriven guitar riff that transforms an already powerful song into a turbulent surge of ecstasy.

At this point in the song Roger had returned to the counter and was now standing supplicant in front of the stereo. His left hand was outstretched in the air carving out signs like a Sufi; his right hand fluttered above the volume control and made occasional micro-adjustments to the sound level. Every plucked bass note and accentuated drum beat compelled Roger to contort his body in time.

His eyes were firmly shut as his head oscillated and shook as if possessed, and I felt a sense of relief that, even though we were without customers, his back was turned.

When the fourteen minutes of 'Yoo Doo Right' drew to

a close in a haze of speaking in tongues Roger's possession subsided.

'Can't have Can on in the shop,' Roger muttered, slowly walking once more towards the back room. 'Can't have it on in here.'

The Revolver infatuation with Can anticipated a rediscovery of German music instigated by the publication of the book *Krautrocksampler: One Head's Guide to the Great Kosmische Musik – 1968 Onwards* by Julian Cope. The *Krautrocksampler* paperback shared the production values of German editions of mystical pulp texts such as Carlos Castaneda's *The Teachings of Don Juan* or Erich von Däniken's *Chariots of The Gods?* with which many Revolver customers were familiar. The cover photograph of *Krautrocksampler*, a reproduction of the sleeve of *Yeti* by Amon Düül that showed the band's stone-faced organist wearing a dress and grasping a scythe in the manner of an initiate, enhanced the sense of street-level doctrine.

As an artist who had wilfully derailed his career only to take charge of it by self-releasing records, publishing books and turning himself into a one-man 'ambassador for looseness', Cope was a folk hero in the shop and among our customers. Head Heritage, the name Cope gave his imprint for *Krautrocksampler*, was a phrase that applied equally to their record collections and curatorial acquisitiveness.

In *Krautrocksampler* Cope wrote with the ardour of an obsessive fan and the authority of a newly appointed professor who has been granted a worryingly free hand. In keeping with his principles of self-reliance and DIY, Cope had made the book available through what in the early 1990s amounted to a series of underground distribution channels consisting of independent record shops and mail order services. Revolver obtained as many copies of *Krautrocksampler* as possible until its print run came to an end.

Apart from Kraftwerk, whose catalogue was owned and managed by EMI, and the rather threadbare CDs we stocked by Can, the majority of the music Cope examined in *Krautrocksampler* was difficult to obtain. Customers increasingly approached the counter with requests for records by Harmonia, Neu! and Cosmic Jokers that were either long deleted or only available on semi-legal and expensive Japanese imports.

In the 'K' section, filed alongside the Can records on the back room wall, were original copies of Harmonia, Neu!, Cluster, Ash Ra Tempel, La Düsseldorf, Popul Vuh and Cosmic Jokers. Several of these albums had been released on the German Brain label, whose logo was a hand-drawn profile over which was superimposed the name 'Brain' written in mountains and clouds. In *Krautrocksampler!* Cope had included images of many of these album covers and now, here under the single bare bulb at the rear of the shop, they were here to be held, studied and contemplated like saintly artefacts.

We began taping our Kosmische musik archive for customers who were asked for a pound surcharge on top of the cost of the TDK SA 90 cassette, and increasing numbers of our regular clientele would leave the shop with a tape of *Deluxe* by Harmonia or Cluster's *Zuckerzeit* in their record bag along with their weekly purchases. For a six-month period Revolver flourished in this souk-like atmosphere of potlatch and off-the-books cultural exchange. There was energy about Roger I had not previously encountered, that derived, I assumed, from being reminded of running the market stall in Portobello Road.

It was accepted and expected that Revolver had a quota of eccentric regulars. To loiter at its counter served as a form of displacement activity for the extended membership of Bristol's artistic and loafing community, whose capacity for spending its spare time scouring record racks was often its most tangible achievement. Although it was an establishment willing to unhesitatingly judge someone by their music purchases, Revolver was incapable of discriminating against the manner in which its customers went about their lives. A customer who had neglected to bathe for a week was given as warm a reception as anyone wearing aftershave or cologne, and both were treated with the same rough-hewn equanimity.

Visitors might arrive at the counter drunk or, as occasionally happened, dressed in clothes that exuded the sickly sweet tang of heroin. In either case their arrival was often followed by a brisk enquiry as to our level of interest in purchasing whichever part of a record collection they might have secreted under their arm.

The only group of customers capable of producing a discernible unease in me, whose approach to the counter forced me to check that my escape route through the back door remained unimpeded, were those who came in search of releases by, or conversation regarding the artist whose one name regularly designated the final letter on the blackboard's alphabet, Frank Zappa.

Revolver stocked the Frank Zappa titles available on vinyl and devoted a section to him in the racks. On the back-room shelves were more records, including long-deleted original copies of *Hot Rats* and *Weasels Ripped My Flesh*. To show these rarities to the Zappa cognoscenti was to invite, even license, an hour-long dialogue about Frank Zappa's guitar technique, composition and, most problematically, his ability as a satirist. These conversations lasted for up to an hour during which the self-restraint of whoever stood behind the counter was tested as if undergoing a cognitive evaluation.

One of the Zappa supporters most trenchantly held beliefs was that Captain Beefheart, a friend of Zappa's since childhood, should be considered an apprentice to the more shrewd composer and that Beefheart's work be regarded in this light. Their argument ran that as Zappa had funded and produced Beefheart's *Trout Mask Replica* and released the double album on his Straight label, it was Zappa's sharp-witted approach to the music industry and generosity that had given Beefheart's career, then a mire of contractual anomalies and managerial problems, a badly needed structure. Furthermore, in 1975 Zappa invited Beefheart to tour with him for a year, guaranteeing him an income and a sense of direction while further attempts were made to reconcile his convoluted legal affairs. In Revolver Frank Zappa enthusiasts delivered treatises of this kind while continually grasping a corner of the counter, often with both hands, and strenuously avoiding any form of eye contact. I became so familiar with this hypothesis that, other than a cursory listen to *Trout Mask Replica*, I was deterred from listening to Captain Beefheart for well over a decade.

Immediately prior to recording *Trout Mask Replica* Beefheart and the members of his Magic Band lived communally at 4295 Ensenada Drive, Woodland Hills, a wooden house in a city suburb in the San Fernando Valley, Los Angeles.

There, over an eight-month period they wrote and rehearsed the music that became the twenty-eight-song double album.

The building they used is known locally as a Girard Tract, one of around 120 cabins originally built in Woodland Hills by Victor Girard Klienberger, the city's founder and first speculative developer.

Girard's business affairs recalled the Old West. As building work began he erected an entire high street, a series of wooden store-front facades whose contents were empty, to attract investors to the 3,000-acre site and give the impression of a lively free-spending community. Girard also founded an equally fallacious country club and local newspaper, and planted his eponymous city (renamed Woodland Hills in 1941 once Girard had filed for bankruptcy) with over a thousand trees. Once the curious investors committed to a purchase Girard illegally sold one-acre lots as the saplings of pepper, cyprus, pine and eucalyptus took root in the arid landscape.

By the autumn of 1968, when Beefheart and the Magic Band moved in to Ensenada Drive, Woodland Hills had been assimilated into the suburban expanse of the Valley, but Girard's trees had given the area a distinct atmosphere and identity. The Magic Band's house was set back from the road and secluded by a pair of towering eucalyptus. A mile north of the Magic Band's house lay the rural hideaways and dirt roads of Topanga, where Neil Young rehearsed with a new band, Crazy Horse. Ten miles further to the west was the self-consciously bohemian and affluent enclave of Laurel Canyon, along whose understated roads Californian singer songwriters were rehearsing a new form of royalty.

While the songs of his contemporaries imagined the bucolic districts of Los Angeles as Eden extant, the more elemental and environmentally aware Beefheart had committed himself to penury and isolation in a workaday suburban backwater. During their residency on Ensenada, Beefheart and his band underwent a psychological form of exile. They rehearsed for up to fourteen hours a day and lived on a subsistence regime of dried pulses bought with food stamps. Apocryphal stories began to circulate of ominous mind games being played and practical jokes turning sour, of already fragile egos being driven to breaking point by Beefheart's singularity and aggressive instincts. The band reached such a poor physical state that members were driven to stealing food from a nearby supermarket. They were duly caught and arrested by officers who assumed they were homeless addicts. Visitors to the house detected an aura that felt unusual even by the standards of 1968.

In 1998 the Revenant label released *Grow Fins*, a rich and carefully assembled box set of Captain Beefheart out-takes and curiosities. In part the project was an attempt to restore credit to the Magic Band members who had assisted and endured Beefheart during the turbulent creation of *Trout Mask Replica*. The third CD of the *Grow Fins* box is titled *Trout Mask House* and contains an hour of fragments, rehearsals and sketches taped during their eight-month residency in Woodland Hills. Some of the pieces are little more than the ambient sound of the room in which they rehearsed. I once compiled a playlist of these tracks, extracts from forgotten tapes that at times sound like little more than recordings of weird air, and stood outside 4295 Ensenada Drive imagining Beefheart and the Magic Band in residence as I watched the squirrels leap between the overgrown trees. As I removed my headphones, some of the found sounds on the *Trout Mask House* recordings – aeroplanes following a flight path overhead, cicadas, children nearby playing – were replaced by their present equivalent.

But there were elements of the sound collage on the tapes that could never be juxtaposed in the present day: the recording of Beefheart's laconic and jocular conversational voice and his blasts on the clarinet and saxophone that must have been strong enough to leak through the windows and on to the quiet residential street below.

At the time of my visit, like much of the property in the area, Beefheart's Girard Tract seemed perpetually to be on and off the market and desperate realtors would sometimes market the building as 'The Trout Mask Replica House'.

A decade later Beefheart was living near his childhood home of Lancaster, California, in the Mojave Desert. His return to the desert had coincided with the release of a trilogy of Captain Beefheart albums that had found him re-invigorated by working with a younger Magic Band and revered by an audience that, unlike his contemporaries in the late 1960s, understood and appreciated his motives.

The final Captain Beefheart album, *Ice Cream for Crow*, was recorded in 1982, after he had returned to live among the creosote bushes, the jackrabbits and coyote of the Mojave in a trailer. Here he resumed painting this environment as he had done as a child. The expressionist canvases that he had produced throughout his recording career were starting to become collectable and were credited to Beefheart's real name: Don Van Vliet. *Green Tom* (1976) had been used as the cover image for the album *Shiny Beast*, a title that describes perfectly many of the inhabitants of Van Vliet's abstract landscapes. In 1985 he staged two major exhibitions at the Michael Werner Gallery in New York and Cologne.

Although the art world initially considered him another refugee from the recording industry who had taken up a paintbrush, Van Vliet maintained that he had begun to paint and sculpt as a child. His large and colourful pieces were a form of American primitive and became compared to the neo-expressionists beloved of Downtown New York in the early 1980s. One of the most striking aspects of his paintings is the expanse of thickly painted white, the endless, brushed-on, empty space. There are certain times of day in the Mojave when the sunshine is so strong and the light so harsh that the air almost becomes visible. When asked by an interviewer if growing up in the desert influenced his work and his relationship with nature he replied, 'No, I think it's because I've always known I'm an animal.' Perhaps Van Vliet was painting what he saw in front of him, or perhaps, whatever he may have said in interviews about his lack of interest in anything intangible, the landscapes and the spirits that populated them lay within.

I knew nothing of Don Van Vliet's work and little about Captain Beefheart's music. I experienced the teenage rapture of finding a new musical hero along with the accompanying compulsion to hear every fragment he had recorded as an adult. Even without the monomania and uninvited homilies of the Frank Zappa fans in Revolver, I would have eventually discovered Captain Beefheart records in the shop and listened to them continually, in the same relentless manner with which we devoured every other form of music in Revolver. Instead I became fully aware of his work at a time in life when such an intense form of recognition has the feeling of magic.

*

Whatever difficulties I experienced conversing with customers whose opinions were as recalcitrant as my own, I learnt to my near peril that it was possible to become complacent standing behind the Revolver counter.

A self-effacing biker who ran a nearby tattoo parlour was a regular customer. He had excellent taste in what had become known as outlaw country music, which he discussed in his quiet but resonant voice. I had once spent an hour engrossed in his explanation of which Merle Haggard albums to listen to, during which he had also recommended

Willie Nelson's *Red Headed Stranger*. I was too young to fully appreciate these endorsements from such a sophisticated source. Secret knowledge was being shared with me; a kind that required a certain kind of lived-in wisdom about what constituted country music that was unavailable to me.

In a moment of idiotic arrogance and lack of judgement I mistook his relaxed manner as an invitation to indulge in the kind of badinage that occasionally gave the shop a bad name. The biker tattooist had come in asking for some bluegrass. I commented that as a genre bluegrass was soft. 'Soft?' he said, the elongated, almost whispered, vowel sounded rather menacing. He lowered his head and began idly flicking through a box of CDs on the counter.

'Soft,' he appeared to be muttering to himself. He suddenly looked up, deliberately caught my eyes and with his reassuring burr a little louder than usual and in a measured pace said, 'I'll take your head off with an axe.'

Roger had appeared by my side. I started to turn towards him before he flatly gave me some advice. 'Don't look at me,' Roger said. 'You're on your own.'

I started apologising with an extravagance that only made the situation more embarrassing. Time may have benevolently erased the memory but in all likelihood I had also begun to cry.

The biker's gaze was still directed towards me with unflinching and troubling intent. 'Soft,' he repeated. 'Soft.' With indiscernible effort his walrus moustache and whiskers separated to reveal a smile. He turned from the counter and left the shop. As he walked his head shook gently.

A few weeks later he returned to the counter and the incident went unremarked as he enquired about the availability on vinyl of *Guitars, Cadillacs, Etc., Etc* by Dwight Yoakam. Later whenever we passed in the street my greeting to him was simultaneously garbled and histrionic and met with the same smile with which he had curtailed his traumatising threat.

One Saturday afternoon I was kneeling behind the counter, filing and reordering stock after a hectic hour and a half during which the shop had enjoyed one of its occasional rushes. As I rose to my feet I was taken aback to see two police officers standing on the other side of the counter. By their body language I hesitantly decided that this was some form of social visit, although their lack of interest in any of the records surrounding them felt ominous. The policeman standing on the left had three stripes on his epaulette that along with his gait, his tattooed forearm and the jangling of loose change in his pocket gave clear indication of his rank. His colleague was a little more upright in his posture. It was difficult to establish what level of seniority he held within Avon and Somerset Police, though he had the look of a man accustomed to being in control, even when standing on the customer's side of the Revolver counter.

The sergeant removed his right arm from his trouser pocket, leant forward and asked if Mr Dogherty was available. I walked towards the back room just as Roger emerged with his usual grin. Not wishing to appear disconcerted by the police he continued towards the turntable and carefully changed the record with customary flourish.

'Hello,' said Roger with the deep-felt enthusiasm and warmth he reserved for aficionados of British jazz.

'Iron Butterfly,' said the sergeant in a fairly thick Bristolian accent.

'Iron Butterfly, Innna Gaaarda Davinaar. That's the one!' he continued, making a great play of having summoned the album's title from memory.

'Bottle-of-scotch album, that is.'

'Is that right?' laughed his superior, before turning to Roger and saying, in a manner suggesting that he was about to make a demand rather than ask a question, 'How are you, Mr Dogherty?'

'Mr Dogherty?' said Roger in disbelief.

'Call him Roger' I interceded, warming to Roger's confidence.

'Have you got Iron Butterfly on CD then, Roger?' asked the sergeant.

For an hour Roger, the two policemen and I maintained this strained and, at times exceptionally circular, conversation during which the occasional customer wandered in and quickly wandered back out. Through the window I could see that it had grown dark. The shop had long passed its usual closing time, but the two policemen still lingered at the counter and even Roger, as accomplished as anyone at maintaining a pointless debate, was starting to show signs of fatigue.

I knew there was no CD copy of *In-A-Gadda-Da-Vida* in stock, but there was likely to be a vinyl pressing on a shelf in the back room. Glad of a reason to leave the counter I deliberately took several minutes to locate the album before returning to pass it to the sergeant.

'That's the one!' he said, smiling. 'Bottle-of-whisky record, this is. Saturday night, sit down with a bottle of whisky, put this one on.'

'Would you like to buy it?' I asked.

'No. I haven't got a record player have I? CD I'm after.'

'I'll buy it then,' said his colleague.

'Give us a tenner,' said Roger.

The transaction completed, the officers left with no further conversation or farewell. With a quicker than usual pace Roger walked into the back room, through the side door and briskly brought the board in from the street before locking the front entrance behind him. He returned to the counter shaking his head. Although temporarily rattled he started to regain his usual poise and I asked him what reason lay behind a police visit of such length. For a few moments his head continued to shake and Roger stared at his feet. He then began to explain the circumstances that had prompted their call. The police had loitered with such deliberate and prolonged presence to remind Roger that recently Revolver had been the subject of a criminal investigation, one that had culminated in a drugs bust.

Eighteen months earlier, a few weeks before I started working at Revolver, the shop had been raided by the police. On a late weekday afternoon, four plain-clothes officers joined two colleagues feigning interest in the record racks and began issuing instructions in loud voices that nobody was permitted to leave the shop. One of the officers vaulted the counter in order to prevent the staff from entering the back room, then being occupied by two of his colleagues.

As the officers started shifting record boxes and dismantling shelves with a matter of fact sense of purpose, everyone present, including a handful of customers, was informed they were likely to be detained in Revolver for the foreseeable future. The operation lasted six hours; the police had seized the shop with an agreed procedure and a search warrant had been presented by the officer in charge upon arrival. As Roger inspected the official documents he noticed that the Thames Valley Police rather than the local force from Avon and Somerset Constabulary were conducting the raid.

The raid had been ambitious in its scope and planning. For a few months the police had commandeered an empty suite above a solicitor's office across the road from the shop entrance for surveillance. From there they had accumulated evidence confirming their suspicions that the buying and selling of records and CDs at Revolver was a pretext for the manufacture and distribution of LSD.

Their supposition was based on an anonymous tip-off left on an answering machine at police headquarters. As officers monitored the shop, the investigation was given a procedural boost by the fact the majority of people entering and exiting Revolver were of the exact physical and psychiatric profile of a typical LSD user. After a month the police had built a case that necessitated a request for operational support from a neighbouring force with experience of drug raids and the date for a raid on Revolver was agreed. Throughout their inspection the police were reasonably courteous and were careful not to damage any stock, although in the hours prior to the raid they had intimidated customers leaving the shop they recognised from their surveillance.

The police managed to conceal their disappointment when the investigation uncovered a negligible amount of marijuana found in the inside pocket of a leather bag kept in the back room and nothing else. Once they realised the shortcomings in their intelligence, the officers dismissed all those held in the shop except Roger and his colleagues who were instructed to accompany them to Broadmead Police Headquarters for interrogation.

Roger asked if he might be able to make the journey himself in his van. The police acceded to the request but explained he would need to be accompanied by an officer.

As was his occasional tendency in the evenings, Roger was experiencing a moment of forgetfulness. Over the years he had turned parking his van on one of the unmetered side streets near Revolver into an art form. so he asked the policeman acting as his chaperone for patience as he attempted to remember on which cul-de-sac or back alley he had left it that morning.

At the time of the bust Roger lived in Cheltenham. He was informed by the police that they had followed him home from Bristol in the preceding months. His postman had once remarked that he suspected Roger's mail was being intercepted and inspected, but neither this comment from the postman nor the police cars on his tail had registered to any effect.

In the early hours of the morning Roger and his colleagues were released from custody. There was a minor charge for possession for the owner of the leather bag who duly neglected to attend the hearing and was rearrested some months later.

3

Revolver opened in 1970 or 1971. The early history of the shop and the names of its founders are sometimes disputed. It is usually agreed that Tony Dodd, a friendly Bristolian and an expert in country and rock 'n' roll, was the shop's first proprietor. Initially Dodd had a business partner, but I have been unable to identify him. As well as running Revolver, Dodd played in local bands and ran stalls at record fairs. Eventually he opened a unit as a sole trader in a market halfway up Park Street. This grew into Tony's Records, a popular store that lasted into the mid-1990s and was one among half a dozen record shops in the Clifton area.

Within a few years of trading Revolver had earned a reputation for stocking the definitive releases of every genre. Rather than trading as a specialist shop, Revolver was regarded as an authority on every style of music. By the mid-1970s it had become the place to buy reggae in particular, a music imbued with unspoken rules and customs of purchase that were enacted at the shop counter in an almost ritualistic manner. Much of the shop's stock of new releases was bought directly from the Jamaican source; a network of vans and drivers used to arrive at Revolver with a selection of current imports, or a wholesaler, Jet Star in Harlesden, provided a regular supply from the studio-owned pressing plants and record shops of Kingston.

There had previously been specialist reggae shops in the city, notably RCA (Record Collectors Association) a father-and-son establishment on Picton Street in Montpelier. The shop sold imported bluebeat and rocksteady singles to a clientele that included suedeheads and local DJs. Another outlet was located in the Bamboo Club in the neighbouring district of St Paul's, an area that had a high concentration of Jamaican residents.

This inner suburb near the city centre had suffered during the Blitz, and many of its inhabitants had been rehoused in new estates built at the edges of the city during the expansion of the 1950s. The area experienced deprivation and a lack of investment during the post-war years, but because of the availability of rented accommodation in its spacious Georgian terraces it became popular with first generation immigrants, many of whom were from the Caribbean.

The Bamboo club opened in 1966 on St Paul Street in the heart of the district. In addition to a concert hall and record stall, the club contained a hairdresser's shop and a restaurant. It was also the headquarters of the Bristol West Indian Cricket Club. As well as performing there, Bob Marley is said to have visited the club regularly on his debut European concert tour in 1973. As roots became a formidable and popular style of reggae in the 1970s, the Mighty Diamonds, Big Youth and Burning Spear were among the artists who played in the Bamboo Club.

Despite the strength and resilience of its community spirit St Paul's was increasingly left bereft of resources by the local authority. This deprivation was accompanied by the commonly felt sense that the area suffered from oppressive treatment at the hands of the police, particularly in their deployment of the 'sus' law that allowed patrol officers to make arrests merely on the grounds of suspicion. It was widely acknowledged that the arrest of black youths was disproportionately high and that they were especially victimised by the police. The tensions within St Paul's extended beyond race lines. Regardless of their class, colour or heritage, its residents often felt that their neighbourhood was purposely being starved of facilities and infrastructure by the city's authorities, who often gave the impression that they regarded the area as little more than derelict.

Along with the Bamboo Club, St Paul's had an informal network of venues and after-hours meeting places, 'blues' clubs that included the Ajax and the Blue Lagoon and cafés, such as the Black and White which served West Indian food twenty-four hours a day. These establishments acted as safe houses and small, self-reliant community centres. They were regarded as spaces where identities were allowed to flourish. The authorities outside the district felt intimidated by the presence of late-night conclaves in St Paul's, and tended to define the activities within them as provocative and largely criminal.

Blues parties were held either in clubs, people's homes or occasionally in an abandoned building. The parties began in the early hours of the morning and finished once they had reached a natural conclusion, regardless of licensing laws or curfews. When the sound system was positioned in a confined interior location such as the front room of a terrace house, the music it broadcast created a nocturnal pulse.

Against the end wall of a street or in the lee of a derelict building, the physical presence of the sound system was of such strength that it transformed its surroundings into a shared sacred space. In plain sight it became a location where the echoes and delays of dub were refracted at a volume and frequency capable of creating a tangible and temporal other.

For the Rastafarian community living in St Paul's, largely comprised of second-generation immigrants coming of age during social and economic difficulties, the sound system represented a locus for renewal. The immediate vicinity of the sound system became, for the duration of its broadcast, an area temporarily free of life's hardships. It represented instead an affirmative, even deified, territory that had formidable presence. Reconditioned speaker cabinets, stripped-back circuit boards and amplifiers specifically constructed to carry single EQ signals were placed in an improvised semicircle on the pavement. The sound system was designed to produce frequencies that were felt rather than heard. For the sound-system operator the desired reaction from the audience was not that they merely danced but that they surrendered themselves to the authority and intensity of the sound.

The rise of the sound system in Britain coincided with the expansion of dub as a creative medium, one that signified a rejection of material conditions and re-imagined reality as a haunted sphere. Across each separate, purpose-built channel, the system took the base constituents of the recording and reproduced them as disparate elements that could be controlled in isolation and manipulated into an exalted form of incantation.

To the crowd moving to the bass lines echoing across the streets, the eeriness and dread of dub represented an ineffable truth. Snatches of roots lyrics whose subject was repatriation and freedom from the yoke of materialism were heard amidst the disorienting instrumental drop-outs. The words hung in the air, reverberating and repeating at the centre of the sound system's abstract and eternal sounding space, their meaning restated as calls to prayer and rebirth.

In an area of deprivation such as St Paul's, hearing the harshness of everyday experience echoed back on oneself by the sound system became a form of resistance. For anyone suffering discrimination from the police or from employers the system represented not merely a form of escape but a means of devotional self-expression.

The records were known as 'pre's, or pre-releases, and dubplates. Rather than finished product for commercial releases, these were acetates or releases limited to a handful of pressings that would be sold or distributed directly to sound-system DJs and controllers. Many of these recordings received their first public air play at 'battles', where rival sound systems would compete for the approval of the crowd, or at parties in the community where visiting systems played new selections. Dubplates and 'pre's that proved their worth in these situations became known as 'weapons'. The implied confrontation in the terms 'battle' and 'weapons' was justified, as police raids on sound systems, which were felt by those attending to be hostile incursions into community relations, were frequent. The system had little use for albums or any recording cut at a frequency spectrum inadequate for its bass bins.

In Bristol one of the richest and most reliable source for 'pre's and dubplates was Revolver.

At the time of the popularity of the sound systems, Revolver's founders had left and the staff now numbered three: Chris Parker, its owner, and two assistants, Lloyd Harris and Mike Chadwick. Revolver had created its own supply chain for 'pre's, dubplates and all other reggae releases, including a van delivery service driven by Adrian Sherwood, one of Britain's most trusted reggae adepts.

Each week a limited number of imported releases would arrive and the sound-system operators would convene at a designated time at the shop's counter to evaluate the delivery. This sale of goods had its own protocol, a form of auction whose procedure had been underwritten and was exclusively understood by the sound-system operators. Within seconds of one of the shop staff playing a new release, an operator would lift a hand to signify their decision to buy the record, which was swiftly removed from the turntable. It was imperative that the record was only heard for as scant few bars as possible, in order that its potency when played on the sound system remained intact. When Revolver was able to buy more than one copy of a record the operator bought the entire supply to ensure its scarcity.

In the streets of Kingston vinyl was created in a closed production line; the studios in which the music was recorded had direct access to the island's pressing plants and on manufacture the records were sold in the studio's own store front.

A handful of the batches of records that had been created by this method would arrive as exported goods at Revolver. The vinyl regularly bore off-centre labels or surface crackles, anomalies that acted as badges of authenticity. Most, but by no means all, imported releases came in a cardboard, or more usually paper, sleeve. The materials used in their construction often had the hallmarks of previous usage such as brand names from cereal packets or other dried foods, reminders that these records were a commodity from and for a specific culture.

The mere act of holding an imported Jamaican 7" made

the street economy of reggae self-evident, as if a natural resource had been extracted at its headspring and exported with as little outside interference as possible.

At the blues parties the Revolver staff were recognised and welcomed. Lloyd Harris told me that his attendance was dictated by stamina after the realisation that the parties often reached their climax at approximately the time he would usually be opening the shop.

In December 1977, on the eve of a Sex Pistols concert it was due to host, the Bamboo Club burned down and an amenity for the entire St Paul's community was lost overnight. The shared spaces such as the Ajax and the community centre that remained took on an added importance in the cultural life of the area. By the late 1970s St Paul's was experiencing disproportionately high levels of unemployment among black school leavers, many of whom often saw their equally or less skilled white contemporaries successfully apply for positions for which they had been rejected.

In 1980 St Paul's rioted. The provocation was presumed to be a dispute between a customer and the police during one of their regular raids on the Black and White café. Many in the community, however, having experienced such enduring oppression, regarded the riot as inevitable rather than as a response to a specific incident.

Analysis undertaken by social scientists concluded that the confrontations with the police had involved people of black, white and mixed race identities. A year later, as the tensions created by the sus law and the overbearing approaches of urban policing gave way to uprisings, many of the British inner cities that hosted and were represented by sound systems also rioted.

In 1982, in response to the Brixton riots in south London, the then Conservative government commissioned the Scarman Inquiry to assess the causes and effects of the disturbances. Following further rioting the inquiry's remit was expanded to include Manchester, Toxteth, Birmingham and Southall. In his report Lord Scarman concluded that 'urgent action' was needed to prevent racial disadvantage becoming an 'endemic, ineradicable disease threatening the very survival of our society'.

During his party conference speech in the autumn of 1981, the Conservative chairman, Norman Tebbit, pre-empted the inquiry's conclusions. With a disdain that was shared by the prime minister, Margaret Thatcher, Tebbit refuted Scarman on grounds of intellectual and societal irrelevance:

I am not willing to throw away the prospects of lasting recovery in an orgy of self-indulgence, false sentimentality and self justification and no one in this government is.

The tone of his peroration grew insistent, as though he felt aggrieved.

The crisis through which we have gone has been a crisis of leadership. The people of Britain are unchanged. They are still the ones who in those immortal words, have met the three corners of the world and shot them. They are strong and they are proud, and we have no right to delude them with a soft options, with the proposition that there is a middle way between right and wrong to suit everyone or to suggest that we escape debt by borrowing more, or hard times by doing less.

One consequence of the Scarman Report, whose findings were largely ignored, was the introduction of 'policing by consent'. This initiative attempted to prioritise community relations above arrest targets and for the first time sound systems were tolerated rather than targeted by the police. In St Paul's, where sound-system battles were regularly held in the newly built Malcolm X Community Centre, the community became partly defined by sound-system culture.

By the time of the first St Paul's riots Revolver had become a member of the Cartel, an affiliation of independent record shops that developed into a parallel national distribution network for music that was considered to be largely irrelevant to the Top 40. Although all seven members of the Cartel supplied their own catalogue of releases into the distribution system, the axis of this supply chain was the Rough Trade label and distribution company in London.

In addition to Bristol and London, Cartel members were

located in York, Leamington Spa, Edinburgh, Liverpool and Norwich. When it functioned at its best, the result of this nationwide infrastructure was an exercise in logistics. Releases that had been recorded and manufactured across the provinces and outside the capital were distributed from the back rooms of a series of record shops to like-minded retailers.

The Cartel was occasionally prone to a certain kind of aspiration. Its members considered its activities to be more than straightforward music retailing and distribution. At its most ambitious, the Cartel regarded itself as an intervening organisation that permitted regional access to a closed-off metropolitan recording industry.

Much of the music the Cartel distributed shared a similar earnestness and experimentalism that on occasion and to unsympathetic ears could sound like the work of amateurs. In particular the bands that played punk or the less orthodox styles that succeeded it comprised much of the Cartel's early catalogue.

Lloyd Harris and Mike Chadwick, formerly just employees, were now Revolver's owners. They had been encouraged to gain control of the shop by the Cartel and to prescribe distinct roles for one another: Harris ran the wholesale and distribution and Chadwick managed the shop. Decisions about which of the local acts appearing increasingly at the Revolver counter seeking finance and distribution from the Cartel should be approved were shared equally.

In a similar manner to other members of the Cartel the shop developed a working relationship with its local punk label, which in Bristol was Heartbeat records. The shop also became involved with two bands whose music was a manifestation of the character and atmosphere of the city at the time.

The first, Talisman, were a mixed-race group financed from the profits of Revolver by its erstwhile owner Chris Parker. The band played a tightly constructed form of roots that they released on the shop's in-house label, Recreational Records. Talisman's position as a popular live act was affirmed at a launch party for their debut single 'Dole Age' held in one of the barns on Michael Eavis's farm near Glastonbury in 1981. In the same year the St Paul's band Black Roots released two singles, 'Bristol Rock' and 'Chanting for Freedom', on their own label, Nubian Records.

The copyright details on Black Roots records included the band's Hepburn Road address in St Paul's, from where for a short period they also ran a record shop. There was an extended symbolism in a band from the area being entirely self-sufficient. Black Roots played conscious music with an intensity that epitomised the district's culture. The resources for producing and manufacturing the band's recordings came from the concerts they regularly gave in front of sound systems, where their performances were its live band equivalent. The low-end frequencies of the system had enough strength to expel the dread felt in everyday life. However Talisman's 'Dole Age' and 'Bristol Rock' were its harsh realities, a Bristolian interpretation of 'sufferation' pressed onto vinyl and introduced by Revolver into the operations of the Cartel.

Whereas its other members regularly contributed releases by trebly guitar bands into the Cartel release pool, Revolver's contribution, inter alia, was Bristol roots music. When it was financing Talisman and distributing Black Roots, Revolver had become a nationwide distributor for reggae. Harris and Chadwick dealt directly with the Greensleeves and Trojan labels and, atypically for an independent shop, had a working relationship with Island, a record company that had attempted, with some success, to transform reggae into an album-centred genre.

Revolver also promoted several artists based in the UK with whom the shop worked on a personal basis. Lloyd Harris regularly drove to the studios and houses of Jah Shaka, Norman Grant of the Twinkle Brothers and Bim Sherman to collect stock. And the shop continued to source reggae directly from Jamaica. Near the bottom of the information sheets of coloured A4 paper Revolver used to list its inventory was written 'Import and pre-release reggae albums available when in season'.

I knew very little about reggae when I started working at Revolver. During my third or fourth week a delivery of Jamaican releases arrived from Jet Star. Every album boasted an arcane title: *Treasure Isle Volume One*, *Ital Dub*, *Rockers Dub*, *Super Dub Disco Style*, *King at the Control*, *Majestic Dub*.

The artwork on these records was rudimentary. The cover designs featured drawings or paintings, occasionally an unsophisticated photographic portrait, and were accompanied by hand-drawn block lettering. The song titles offered little information and usually consisted of one word followed by 'Dub' or one of its variants: 'Jack a Dub', 'Lion Dub', 'The Heights Dub', 'The Aggrovators', 'Special Dub', 'Everybody Dubbing'. A short sentence of information was written below the track listing, usually stating 'recorded at King Tubby's'; in only a few instances this also included a date.

In terms of their physical condition the records felt similar to bootlegs. The sleeve of *Treasure Isle Dub* had the same thick card texture as an egg box and its inside also contained artwork. In my curiosity I took the record into the back room and held the sleeve under a bare light bulb to inspect these hidden designs more carefully. Gradually the words 'Air Jamaica' began to emerge amid the blue, yellow and orange red lines that I assumed formed part of the airline's insignia.

The raw materials that had been accumulated to manufacture *Treasure Isle Dub* had been chosen out of expediency rather than any other factor. Instead of a standard white polythene-lined inner sleeve, the vinyl came housed in a hastily assembled plastic casing that was as wafer thin as cling film. It was possible to see the stitches that had been used in its construction, presumably on a domestic sewing machine.

The record itself had slightly off-centred labels and a few drops of melted plastic had solidified near the centre hole. Once I had placed it on the turntable I was struck by the vivacity of the music. After a few bars the bass line was firmly established and I noticed a mild tremor had appeared in the shop's speakers. The sound was warm, rich and direct. Although I knew dub was considered to be a genre suited for the immediacy of either the 'version' of a 7" B side or for the dubplates, acetates and 12"s cut specifically at 45 rpm for its enhanced volume capacity, the power and directness of the album playing over the shop's system was all pervading. I realised, by the mere act of shaking my head along in time to the bass while standing at the counter, that this was a music created for physical experience.

Within a week the delivery of imported stock had all been sold. As I expressed an interest in their purchases, some customers offered me advice on how to develop an affinity with reggae records.

'The worse the sleeve looks, the better the record,' suggested a regular in a suit, who always visited the shop during his office lunch break.

'The sign of a good album is one with more than one sleeve. If you've seen the same record with two or three different covers, that means it's had to be repressed a few times, so it's popular, and the people have voted with their wallets.'

It was also explained to me that, as there was very little copyright law in Jamaica, finished songs and their backing tracks known as 'riddims' were bought and sold as commodities or perishable goods. I was surprised at the depth of feeling many of our customers had for reggae, and for dub in particular.

While listening to an album credited to 'King Tubby's' I developed a theory that might explain the music's popularity.

For all its reputation as a city that was perpetually stoned, I began telling Roger, and putting its West Indian diaspora aside for one moment, – I added, to his obvious incredulity – Bristol was perhaps a city that suited reggae's rhythms. As I began to elaborate on this idea I noticed that Roger, with complete justification, was now walking away, his head shaking, almost in pity.

Roger had had some unique experiences in retailing reggae. In a delivery of imported releases similar to those I had recently unpacked, he had once found a cache of a thousand dollars. Some days later some atypical and rather threatening customers made enquiries concerning a consignment from Jamaica. Their presence in the shop and the manifest disregard that they displayed towards the stock suggested at best only a passing interest in music. Nevertheless, Roger suggested they look in the dub section, as that was the likely location of any recently imported stock. The body language with which Roger's advice was met only confirmed the urgency of their visit to Revolver, although their dropped shoulders and unwavering eye contact suggested a slim probability of a desire to purchase. They left the shop empty-handed but the sense of menace remained.

On another occasion, two concert promoters paid an impromptu visit to Revolver that resonated with Roger far more deeply. The majority of concert promoters viewed Revolver and the neighbouring record shops on Park Street as reliable points of sale. Roger was agreeable to selling most concert tickets in Revolver, and as he accepted the book of tickets from a promoter, he would habitually pass on an affable and often discerning assessment of the integrity and viability of the line-up.

A ticket book for a forthcoming lovers rock concert had been accepted in the customary manner; the venue for the performance was a short-lived exhibition centre in an old dockyard near the harbour front.

The area had yet to be redeveloped. As illegal warehouse parties were also occasionally staged nearby there was an added frisson and air of expectation to the event.

On the day before the performance the concert's promoter visited Revolver and asked to collect any monies and ticket receipts owed. Roger duly calculated the value of the sales and gave the promoter several hundred pounds and the remainder of the unsold tickets. As reggae concerts usually attracted a 'walk-up' audience, that is one that is happy to purchase tickets at the door, the book of tickets Roger returned to the promoter was of significant value.

The following morning Roger was briefly disconcerted when two men arrived at the counter and announced that the purpose of their visit was to collect the money due on ticket sales for that evening's concert at the Bristol Exhibition Centre. As he explained to the visitors that he had settled with the promoter the previous day, Roger sensed their growing agitation and summoned the nerve to remain calm as they insisted they be allowed into the back room to resolve the matter. This was an instruction rather than a request and one, Roger noted, that was accompanied by a gesture by one of the visitor's that indicated he was armed.

For the first time in Revolver's history, a tense and ominous atmosphere in the back room was attributable to something other than an argument concerning an obscure record. Alone with the two men, who had now started to bristle with annoyance, Roger sensed that any attempt to explain that he may have been defrauded by a rogue concert promoter the previous day was futile. In response to their repeated demands to provide a description of the imposter, Roger insisted he had a poor memory for faces. His interrogators however, despite protestations that he was unlikely to recognise their suspect, determined that they and Roger should, at that moment, drive to St Paul's and begin a manhunt.

Instructions were given to lock up the shop. Within a

few seconds of closing the door, Roger was led towards a BMW parked directly outside the shop door. The man Roger assumed to be armed was now wearing a long leather coat and held one of its rear doors open. After a ten-minute drive Roger and his captors arrived in St Paul's. There they undertook a tour of shebeens and venues, including the Ajax and the Black and White café, in the hope of identifying and confronting the rogue promoter. Although he was wary of his two kidnappers, Roger sensed that their interest in him was financial rather than personal. In spite of this, the chances of locating their suspect remained slight and he grew nervous as he imagined the possible consequences.

At every card table they interrupted, Roger's captors met little resistance. With a growing awareness that men with reputations had abducted him, Roger explained that, true to his word, he was unable to recognise the imposter that had visited Revolver. For a further hour Roger was led through the back doors of corner cafés and up the dimly lit stairwells of pubs until it was agreed he and the two men would return to Revolver.

In Roger's unexplained absence the shop had been reopened by a member of staff, who was now suddenly disconcerted to see Roger walk into Revolver accompanied by two men whom at first sight he mistook for bodyguards. Roger was informed that the shop was to be emptied and he once again found himself alone in the shop with two frustrated and intimidating strangers.

They explained their interpretation of the facts to Roger; yesterday's transaction was to be rescinded and he now owed the value of the ticket sales in full. It was near the end of trading hours and Roger explained to the visitors that, as so little cash had been taken due to the shop's unexpected closure, payment would only be possible the following day. They were welcome, he explained, to try his bank card in a cash point, but if they did so they would find themselves empty-handed. Keen to arrive at the concert venue before the doors opened, the promoters agreed to Roger's terms. They would return the following afternoon once they had concluded any outstanding business arising from that evening's show.

Perplexed and tired by the day's events, but determined to avoid having to settle a set of ticket sales twice, Roger began to think on his feet. In their haste to appear threatening and ready to undertake a manhunt the two promoters had neglected to ask Roger for the exact figures that had changed hands and had settled on using the term 'the money' for the sum they insisted they were owed. Roger realised that if he forged a handwritten sales receipt from the fraudulent transaction and reduced the amount that he had given the impersonator, his liability could at least be diminished.

The spontaneous mounds of paperwork and botched invoices that seemed to form of their own volition provided Roger with ample material to forge a receipt. He tore a neat strip of card and wrote the name of the concert, the date and a figure that was close to two-thirds of the amount he had paid. Near the bottom, in different ink, he wrote CASH and the appropriate numbers. With the same pen, but now held between his thumb and third finger, he drew an indecipherable signature. The counterfeit receipt was then folded and gently rubbed across the shop counter in an improvised, though immediately effective, ageing process.

At two o'clock the following day the two men returned. Their malevolent demeanour had hardened overnight and Roger welcomed them with businesslike haste. In a single movement he handed them the forged sales receipt and began counting out the amount, £300, in used ten-pound notes. In the instant after the money had changed hands the promoters left Revolver without conversation or further instructions. The shop phone had been ringing with more regularity than usual and having ignored it, as he sometimes did, Roger began to answer the calls. Several customers were ringing with a similar complaint. They had bought tickets for the previous evening's concert and wanted to register their disappointment that the show had been cancelled and wondered whom they should approach for a refund.

The original visitor to the shop, who had claimed to be the promoter, the two men eager to pursue him and the concert itself had all been fraudulent. Roger was left wondering to what degree he had been involved in a minor criminal exercise. The identity of the three imposters was never known, nor was this the final instance of a reggae concert in Bristol being cancelled for unresolved reasons at short notice. Given the distance, fragility and volatility of its domestic music industry, the non-appearance of a reggae performer at a publicised concert was a calculated risk accepted when purchasing a ticket. I had experienced cancellations across all musical genres and assumed the city was considered unimportant in comparison to Glasgow or Manchester.

In my naivety the idea of a concert being an entire fiction and a ruse to generate a fast income from the turnover of false ticket sales seemed fantastical. The fact that two separate factions had contested the ownership of its proceeds seemed to elevate the idea from a scam into a form of bootleg theatre. Although Roger's kidnapping was a story that was recounted quietly over the ensuing years, it illustrated the extent to which Revolver was unregulated, and how at times the lack of systems, checks and balances might become a liability. Our operating procedure remained relaxed whichever other parties were involved, whether armed or not.

Revolver lacked a chart-return machine, so the shop was without the facility for registering sales. Reps for major labels thus neglected to include Revolver on their promotional rounds. Independent distributors were a separate matter, though; when answering the phone we recognised their voices. If a new release or back catalogue item they felt might be of interest to us arrived at their warehouse, they would make an exceptional call to inform us. However irregular its cash flow, Revolver remained one of their most significant clients and the stock from the independent distributors was our lifeblood.

I noticed that, compared to the era when the shop was a distributor and member of the Cartel and a retailer, the sense of being an alternative to the mainstream record business was absent. To make such distinctions had become a minority interest. The greater part of the stock we carried from smaller distributors, particularly releases imported from America such as 7" singles on small American labels, was rarely covered in the weekly music press.

I was surprised one day to receive a lunchtime phone call from a sales rep at Polydor. As the label owned and distributed the Island catalogue, we were accustomed to placing orders with Polydor every few weeks. Our relationship with the company was perfectly formal and orthodox but we rarely received visits from their reps or regular calls from their telesales staff. Island's mid-price Reggae Greats series included titles by Burning Spear and Lee Perry, which were items that sold regularly and often constituted the bulk of our shipments. They had also provided some of our less adventurous customers – and myself – with the bedrock of a reggae education.

'I'm ringing as we have a new label,' the rep began, 'and I think it's one you're going to do well with there. You're probably going to be really into it.' The first reaction to any such statement in the shop was to register one's disbelief that anyone could be so presumptuous. The genuine sense of excitement in the rep's voice notwithstanding, I was struck by his professionalism and that he was obviously prepared to suffer what were likely to be replies of hostility and abuse in the name of carrying out his promotional duties.

'Oh. Right,' I said.

'Yes, it's a new reggae label. I say new – what I mean is, it's a new label that is going to be doing really serious reissues of some of the obscure roots stuff.'

'Oh. Right. I see,' I said. I started to enjoy our exchange and began also a mental evaluation of why a major label might be inclined to involve itself in such a promising sounding project. Before I was able to articulate my concerns the rep provided me with an explanation.

'It's being done by Simply Red,' he said.

Although I suspected this statement was an extension of his customary sales pitch. it had a rather deflating effect on our conversation. What had for a moment seemed to be a rare instance of corporate money financing a series of worthy and engaging archival releases was, at the mention of the name Simply Red, revealed, in my mind at least, to be an act of whimsical indulgence on the part of the record company. A chief executive had presumably been instructed to undertake whatever action was required to ensure the happiness of one of their highest-grossing acts. If only they had considered the consequences. Assured in my judgement, I ordered a handful of the label's first release and felt a slightly grudging acceptance that in 'Blood and Fire' this new venture had an accomplished and suitable name.

The first Blood and Fire release, *If Deejay Was Your Trade*, was a compilation of singles from the mid-1970s. Its subtitle, 'The Dreads at King Tubby's', captured the atmospheric sound of the album: Jamaican DJs – artists who sang or declaimed over previously recorded rhythms – describing daily life in Kingston through the perspective of their Rastafarian beliefs. The tracks were created by the producer Bunny 'Striker' Lee, 'King Tubby's' being the studio where Lee had made the recordings. Osbourne Rudduck, or King Tubby as he and his sound system had become known, had utilised his knowledge of radiogram engineering to build a studio and working environment where the recording of dub had become a scientific process.

This process was examined in *Dub Gone Crazy*, the second Blood and Fire release that arrived within a few weeks of *If Deejay Was Your Trade* and instantly joined the Revolver canon. The artwork from the original 7" singles from which many of the Blood and Fire releases were compiled was featured on the album's reverse sleeves. Their labels might feature handwriting or smudged print work, and in most cases the producer on their own imprint released them in small runs. In 1976, if they had left Jamaica as exports, one of their intended destinations might well have been Revolver.

Within three years the label had released sixteen faultless

albums of Jamaican roots music with a rare assurance and authority. Each release was mastered with a clarity that allowed the profound nature of the music to breathe and was accompanied by striking artwork and sleeve notes written by the label's founder Steve Barrow. These notes were a biography and meditation on the album's creation and often featured an interview with the record's creator transcribed in their dialect. Reading this patois, I was struck how it was the first time I had read an attempt to convey the tone and grain of the voice of a Jamaican artist without it appearing awkward, gauche or patronising.

As well as compiling sets of a producer's recordings, Blood and Fire reissued original albums. In the case of titles such as *Social Living* by Burning Spear or *Heart of the Congos* by the Congos, the label had taken temporary ownership of the master tapes and had improved on the original releases. They accomplished this by fine-tuning the EQ on each recording; the subtleties and details in every instrument were given a renewed space in which to breathe which resulted in a sharpened audio clarity. I was once told that on *Social Living* Blood and Fire had discovered instruments and vocals on the quarter-inch tape they received from Island Records that had previously been lost or buried in the mix originally released. In the case of *Heart of the Congos*, the Blood and Fire edition of the album was probably the seventh version of the album to be made available. The clarity with which they had mastered the record ensured that as the drum machine of 'Congoman' played on the Revolver stereo it felt as though the shop was about to levitate.

The label also reissued albums that were far less well known. Two titles on its catalogue *Tappa Zukie in Dub* and *In the Light Dub* by Horace Andy had originally been released in editions as few as five hundred.

To listen to the catalogue was a form of higher education. As I turned their records over I began to differentiate between the direct pavement rhythms of Tappa Zukie and the intensity of Yabby You. Although their albums often credited the same groups of musicians, the producers had fashioned distinct sonic identities. I scoured the song titles of the fourth Blood and Fire release *King Tubby's Prophecy of Dub* by Yabby You and was taken aback by their emotional immediacy: 'Anti-Christ Rock', 'Beware of God', 'Hungering Dub', 'Homelessness'.

The sleeve notes, written by Steve Barrow, explained that Yabby You, or Vivian Jackson, was familiar with the writings of Saint John the Divine in the final book of the Bible and its vision of Armageddon.

The music had a mystical lightness and an intensity that was overwhelming. As I was playing the record, a local reggae DJ and promoter, a white man with dreadlocks, came in and stood by the counter. Enraptured by the record we both leant on the counter. He rested on his elbow as he stared, lost in the rhythm. My hand, I realised had become fixed to the surface of the counter as though needing to grasp something solid.

'This is pretty roots,' I said, embarrassed that I lacked the vocabulary to articulate what we were experiencing and intimidated, slightly, by the concentration with which my companion was listening. He nodded his head in time to the music with a growing intensity. Slowly he attempted to respond to my remark – it was a response that seemed to arrive in his consciousness a minute or so after I had spoken.

'Blood roots,' he said quietly. 'Blood roots.'

The first album Blood and Fire reissued was *Pick a Dub* by the producer Keith Hudson. The record's front-cover artwork included a copy of the original version: a line drawing of a man smoking under a palm tree, as the words 'Pick a Dub' appear written on a cloud of smoke that he exhales.

Roger had stowed a collection of reggae albums in a redundant stairwell to the right of the counter. Intrigued and stimulated by reading the Blood and Fire sleeve notes I picked through the records, recognising many of the artists' names for the first time. Near the end of the row I noticed the faded brown colour and naive design of the original *Pick a Dub* artwork, although on the version in my hand some colours and shading had been arbitrarily added in. I turned the record over and studied the label information, the copy I was holding had been manufactured by Atra Records of Lower Clapton Road in Hackney.

Released in 1974 *Pick a Dub* is a collection of sparse,

almost minimal, drum and bass tracks. It is often regarded as one of the first records to be released as a dub album, although the spatial dimensions created by effects such as delay or reverb are used sparingly; instead, the instruments are left to breathe and pulse. The sound of *Pick a Dub* is both earthy and ethereal but its most distinctive characteristic is the sense that it has been created in the moment; as if, over a spare few hours, the producer had bought some studio time and worked by instinct with whatever instrumental tracks were to hand. A hustler's feeling for opportunism can be heard in the fades and edits that lend the album its authority and brooding momentum.

In the row of vinyl near *Pick a Dub* was another record by Hudson. Its cover, in stark contrast to the airy drawing of *Pick a Dub*, featured a black-and-white photograph of what I assumed to be a refugee camp being patrolled by armed guards. I studied it further and grew increasingly confused. What I thought had been a crowd gathering under curfew now looked as though they might be at a dance. There were also three photographs of Hudson superimposed in the sleeve's corners, and staring out from the centre was a smaller picture, of a mother cradling a baby in a moment of heightened maternal affection. Printed across these images were lines of verse that I assumed to be the album's title and that helped explain this last image:

The Black Breast
Has Produced Her
Best,
Flesh of My Skin,
Blood of My
Blood

The back of the sleeve contained several sentences that I struggled to comprehend, underneath which was one single word in block capitals:

STRUGGLE

In the liner notes to the Blood and Fire edition of *Pick a Dub* I had read a reference to an album released in 1975 and titled *Flesh of my Skin, Blood of My Blood* and its 'unique vision and militant consciousness'.

As I let the stylus drop on to the album I felt a shiver of anticipation. The record began and the sounds I heard felt desolate. In comparison to the sidewalk confidence of *Pick a Dub* and its assertive bass lines, these new rhythms and textures were distorted and fragmentary.

The first track, 'Hunting', started with a willowy guitar motif and an echoing harmonica that was reminiscent of 'Gris Gris' by Dr John. Within a few bars the Rastafarian percussion of Count Ossie started marking out a Nyabinghi drum pattern, the watery tone of which was accentuated by the addition of a rain stick.

Without having read the Blood and Fire sleeve notes I would have assumed that I was listening to the work of a different artist named Keith Hudson. The following track began with a piano vamp and for the first time I could clearly hear Hudson's voice. He sounded racked, as though he were stretching for the notes out of an emotional need. From the snatches I could distinguish on first listening, the words he was singing were equally troubled:

> So tired, she want a rest,
> Flesh of my skin, blood of my blood.
> If only you were like my brother that sucked the black breast of my mother.
> Flesh of my skin,
> Blood of my blood,
> Rise up, seen her children grow, she'll see them die.
> Oh, how she cried.
> She has produced her best.

Hudson maintained this level of emotional intensity throughout the album.

As he sang about family, loss and self-doubt, the threadbare confidence in his voice was frail and reinforced by the song titles he had chosen: 'Testing of My Faith', 'Darkest Night', 'My Nocturne'. While listening to Rastafarian music I had been made conscious of the pain and of the desire for a flight from such sufferation that were central to the songs' messages of consciousness. These messages were usually sung with an absolute faith in the ability of the communal to transcend the individual and in the repatriation of an exiled people, a people that described itself in highly masculine, often warrior-like terms. I had never before heard such doubts voiced by an individual on a roots album, nor heard an identity undergoing such a series of crises.

The personal grievousness of *Flesh of My Flesh* proved hard for many listeners to bear. Hudson had recorded much of the music in London and struggled to export the album back to Jamaica for release. Instead a handful of the tracks proved popular with the sound systems in Dalston and Tottenham where he settled before emigrating to New York.

Once there he regularly recorded and released music. At one point Hudson signed a lucrative contract with Virgin Records to produce an album for their Front Line reggae imprint, although the record he delivered, *Too Expensive*, contained a bewildering set of songs performed and recorded in the manner of a soul artist.

He then continued to produce albums on his own Joint International label and once more experimented with the conventions, such as they were, of the reggae music business. In a reversal of the established protocol he produced the dub record *Brand* in 1977, the year before he released its vocal counterpart, *Rasta Communication*.

In a pile of forgotten papers that sat on the same shelf as

Roger's stock of roots and dub albums I found an information sheet from the days when Revolver had been a distributor.

I assumed that this list had originally been typed in the back room before being included in the delivery shipments dispatched from the shop. It listed two sections, 'Albums' and 'Reggae'. Under the second heading I noticed the word 'pre' written after several titles including *Rockers Almighty Dub* and *Unconquered People*. I then smiled in recognition of the next name to be included on the inventory: Keith Hudson *Nuh Skin Up* (Joint International). I remained hopelessly naive about reggae and assumed the title to be a reference to smoking drugs. Some months later it was explained to me that it was a call to arms, to toughen up and display some courage.

During the same conversation I was informed that Keith Hudson had personally delivered these copies of the album to Revolver. He had stood at the counter and struck a deal in a similar manner to the methods he would have used at any record store in Kingston. I was told that this had been a fairly common occurrence in the shop during the late 1970s and early 1980s; that many of the artists released by Blood and Fire, Burning Spear, Yabby You, Tappa Zukie, U Roy and Prince Far I, had all once stood at the counter, in fellowship and in negotiation, and during this conversation I began to wonder if my thoughts about Revolver being situated on hallowed ground were no longer fanciful.

4

There was a room at the rear of Revolver that resembled a cave. It lacked daylight or any source of light other than a single lamp socket precariously attached to the ceiling. Its walls of whitewashed stone regularly glistened with damp and its position within the building suggested that it had originally been used as a coal cellar. For several years it had been the office and warehouse of Revolver Distribution.

On one of my first working days at Revolver I was informed that this abandoned space and its contents still technically belonged to the shop's former proprietors. I glanced at the interior of the room and instinctively reached for the light switch but then realised that the overhead fitting lacked a bulb. As my eyes grew accustomed to the darkness of this cavern I felt them widen at the sight of the thousands of records stacked against its dripping walls in sad, makeshift rows separated by disintegrating cardboard boxes.

The records were excess or remaindered stock left behind by the distribution company following a move to new, larger premises. I picked up a handful of singles strewn in a heap close to my feet. The sleeves were rippled and stained yellow from water damage but their artwork remained visible. Each record I held had been made by a different band, but the lettering and designs on the sleeves were consistent with the inexpensive production values of local acts who had self-released what they felt had been their strongest, or most popular song as a 7" single. A decade later they remained forgotten in this subterranean room, left to atrophy among the gentle drops of condensation that had fallen over the years.

Water had an unpredictable and ominous presence in the shop. Pipes situated behind one of the walls regularly froze during cold winters and burst with enough force to soak through to the area where second-hand records were displayed. In an ill-fated attempt to create a display area for T-shirts, a nail was once struck directly into a downward pipe that ran parallel to the counter. A steady torrent spouted on to the staff and rather than being placed on sale the T-shirts and other random items of clothing were piled against the wall in an attempt to staunch the flow.

The most dramatic incident involved the fire brigade. Revolver's landlord lived above the shop in the large, rather seedy, Georgian townhouse. His hearing was weak, and he was also forgetful. One afternoon, during a particularly hot summer, water fell through the Revolver ceiling. Roger gathered the few available buckets, plastic bowls and empty paint tins, and placed them on the floor underneath the largest drops, while smaller drops continued to land on the shop surfaces. Within an hour water had gathered on the floorboards of the first floor and breached the ceiling, allowing a steady stream to reach the shop.

In vain Roger insistently knocked on the landlord's door and rang his number until, after an hour without any response, he called the emergency services. Within a few minutes a fire engine parked outside the shop and raised its ladder to a window in the town house. The fireman used his axe to gain access to the building and having climbed through the window saw that a bath had overflown and flooded an entire landing in the property.

In the intervening minutes between calling the fire brigade and the fireman draining the bath water, Roger fetched a large, thin tarpaulin from his van. In an attempt to preserve the stock he secured the sheet across the record dividers with lengths of rope and for a few moments, as drops of water were caught in the small patch of sunlight from the window and the shop lights were reflected in the tarpaulin, Revolver bore a resemblance to a barge passing through a lock.

Like my colleagues before me I found it difficult not to examine the water-damaged stock in the stone-walled back room. The first impression, that its contents were discarded from a previous age when local enthusiasm was rewarded with very basic record deals, proved correct. At the front of the room a row of boxes containing singles by West Country acts with shared band members was arranged alphabetically in a forlorn remnant of order.

There were other, less prosaic-looking records scattered among them. Included in the contents of a large cardboard box were three copies of a mysterious album whose sleeve featured a photograph of two Edwardian women. The record covers were warped and the damp had mottled the card in a manner that accentuated the wistfulness of the image. On the sleeve, encircled by a heraldic shield, was written 'Deux Filles' and underneath 'Silence and Wisdom'.

I regarded one of the albums closely and realised that I had been deceived. The two people in the cover photograph wearing pinafores and ribbons in their hair were not Edwardian ladies but young men in drag. I turned the album over. According to what readable text remained the record had been released in 1982, on Papier Mâché records, and was based on the lives of Claudine Coule and Gemini Forque, two girls who had been orphaned and passed unhappy lives. I was familiar with one of the names listed in the credits, Simon Fisher Turner, whom I associated with film music. I assumed these three forgotten copies of the record had once formed part of a consignment delivered to the ill-lit back room.

As I withdrew the record from its sleeve to place it on the turntable, I smiled at one of the printed labels on the vinyl. It featured a photograph of a small boy laughing as he was suspended by his clothes from a washing line. I played the record but struggled to place the music. The short instrumental pieces were fragmentary and immersed in a cloud of echo from which incorporeal voices emerged then retreated with unnerving suddenness.

At other times the music sounded as though it were borrowed from a chamber piece and rescored for an ethereal ensemble of recorded whispers and ticking clocks.

There was a dreamlike solemnity to the music that suggested Fisher Turner and his partner Colin Lloyd Tucker, a sound engineer, had assumed the characters Claudine and Gemini while recording the album, and that the ghosts of *les deux filles* inhabited the songs.

'Silence and Wisdom' had been made in a small four-track studio in Soho that was often used in the recording of film soundtracks. For a fortnight I returned to 'Silence and Wisdom' until its textures and resonances became familiar. At the time the nearest comparison I could draw was to the EPs that Cocteau Twins had recorded for 4AD, although the music Fisher Turner and Lloyd Tucker had recorded was more abstract and more disconcerting.

I was aware that this style of music, meditative, studio-composed and processed, had been given the name 'Ambient Music' by Brian Eno and that the first ambient record *Ambient 1: Music for Airports* was precisely that.

There was a discernible difference between the sound quality of the recordings but the music of Deux Filles and 'Music For Airports' shared a calming quality.

Beneath the veneer of functionality Eno had used for his music was a bucolic tranquillity. This characteristic was only revealed by concentrating on the subtle shifts in composition and production, an activity that was contradictory to Eno's declared intention that the pieces be considered utilitarian and superficial. '1/4', the first composition on *Music for Airports*, features a cyclical piano part played by Robert Wyatt. After repeatedly listening to its opiate cadences I involuntarily heard this piece of music in a separate context from that described by the album title.

The piano part played by Wyatt had been slowed down to roughly half its original speed and set within a perpetual wash of bell chimes, reverberating bass notes and a subtle haze of effects suggestive of a sigh.

Played through the tannoy at an airport the music would doubtless provide a soothing distraction. Listened to intently in solitude, the air circulating around each note of '1/4' grew audible, as if the pianist was following the instructions given by Satie for the playing of his three *Gymnopédies*: '*Lent et douloureux*', '*Lent et triste*', and '*Lent et grave*'.

I listened to '1/4' with such intensity and frequency that I was incapable of hearing this circulation of air as anything other than Arcadian. I imagined it as a mist at the onset of dusk on a clear day, the particular atmosphere Eliot describes in 'Burnt Norton' as 'Smokefall'.

*

In the spring of 1982 the classically trained multi-instrumentalist Virginia Astley began making arrangements to produce an album, a recording that evoked the duration of a day in high summer from morning to nightfall. Astley had written the phrase 'Sweet Third-Deep Grass' in her notebook, from a memory of fielding at Third Deep during a game of rounders, a position where the ball is rarely in play and, unless playing against a strong team, the opportunity to become momentarily invisible and sedate among the long grass is assured.

Astley spent part of her childhood near the village of Moulsford in Oxfordshire where her father, a composer of film and television soundtracks, worked in a small recording studio-cum-study installed in the garage of the family home. An agreement was made that Astley could use this studio for part of the recording which, together with her degree from the Guildhall School of Music, gave her the confidence to recreate the passing of a day in the English countryside. She was also encouraged in the idea by Bill Drummond, who suggested he could release the finished recording on his Zoo record label.

She hired a portable Uher quarter-inch tape recorder and with her partner Russell Webb made field recordings of the wildlife and atmosphere of the Thames Valley. The idea for the record, to be titled *From Gardens Where We Feel Secure*, was highly original, although two records, she told me many years later, may have had subconscious influences.

The first was the 1971 recording of composer Gavin Bryars about a homeless man near Elephant and Castle singing 'Jesus' Blood Never Failed Me Yet', a song whose origins remain unknown. Bryars edited the verses into a thirteen-bar loop that fell in slightly ragged 3/4 time. He used this discrepancy in meter to great effect by adding an orchestral accompaniment to the verse that accentuates the frailty inherent in the voice. The strings and brass in his arrangement rise and fall with an evenness so overwhelming it is difficult for the listener not to grow tearful. The original recording of 'Jesus' Blood Never Failed Me Yet' was released on Eno's Obscure record label in 1975, three years before *Music for Airports*, the other subliminal influence on *From Gardens Where We Feel Secure*.

The music was written in the same key as the field recordings Astley made. These tapes of wildlife and rural hubbub were then cut and edited by hand into loops. Side one of the album, the 'Morning' side, begins with the dawn chorus recorded at 5.30 a.m. on Sunday 25th April; the title of this first piece, 'With My Eyes Wide Open I'm Dreaming', establishes the record's somnambulant character as the birdsong is accompanied by Astley playing piano and flute. The piano part was then run backwards and added to the mix, a process that was repeated through much of the record and contributes to its unearthly atmosphere.

'A Summer Long Since Past', the piece that follows, is one of the few instances of vocals being used on the record. The wordless singing was by Astley and her eldest niece; their voices are in a high register and float behind the instruments as if sung by wood sprites.

The church bells recorded on the late afternoon of 6th June are a feature of the title track that follows. The tower to which they belonged could be seen from Astley's family home. At the end of this piece Astley's younger niece, who was in the room nearest the studio, can be heard crying. As her sobs were in tune it was decided not to erase them from the tape. Elsewhere in the piece the sound of a door being closed, recorded by accident, can also be faintly heard.

The final track on the 'Morning' side is titled 'Hiding in the Ha-Ha'. Astley played a melody on the flute that was slowed to half speed, then pitched an octave higher and is heard as a motif throughout the song that concludes with the soft braying of Lilac, a donkey.

The 'Afternoon' side begins with 'Out on the Lawn I Lie in Bed' (the first line of Auden's *A Summer Night*). The melancholy sound of a gate swinging on its hinges is heard through much of the piece, accompanied by xylophone and echoing piano lines.

A loop formed from the baaing of sheep, a noise that always sounds impatient or impudent, is heard on 'Too Bright for Peacocks' and is offset by the record's most affecting piano part.

The inherent eeriness in the record grows more conspicuous in the album's final three tracks, as the hot afternoon of the day gives way to evening.

'Summer of their Dreams' is created from a tape loop of an oar creaking in its rollocks and brushing the surface water of the river. Many of the instruments added to the tape are played backwards. The overall effect is to suggest to the listener that while making their field recordings, Astley and Webb inadvertently captured the sound of a ghost river man rowing along the rural Thames.

'When the Fields Were on Fire' derives from a dream of Astley's mother in which she saw stubble burning on a hill on the other side of the valley grow out of control. As her mother recounted the dream one morning, the Astley family heard fire engines driving in the direction of the same fields as in the dream. The sound of a telephone can be heard ringing in the piece, as can voices that carried across the water as Astley recorded the bells near the river.

From Gardens Where We Feel Secure concludes with 'It's Too Hot to Sleep'. The hooting of an owl recorded on Sunday 16th May is heard in counterpoint to a piano and rueful flute that fade slowly until the owl, a recording of electronic crickets and the ticking of Astley's father's study clock linger briefly, unaccompanied by instruments, before growing silent.

The nature and wildlife recordings Astley and Webb made on the portable tape recorder dated from the spring,

25 April in particular, a day that falls roughly a month after the vernal equinox. There is a sense that the sadness often felt during an English spring, a sadness that the light is starting to extend and in doing so is leaving one behind, was captured in these field recordings and their contents are filtered with vernal melancholy.

The eerie, otherworldly presence of *From Gardens Where We Feel Secure* in the listener's imagination is partly explained by this elision of recordings of the spring countryside that is used to evoke the serenity of a day in high summer, as if the rhythm and progress of the seasons had been altered.

In the year following its recording the album was released on 29th July, a fitting date for music of such reverie.

As Astley composed the music to accompany the field recordings made for *From Gardens Where We Feel Secure*, Brian Eno was recording his own evocation of an English rural childhood. The fourth album in the Ambient series, *On Land*, was an interpretation of his memories of the Suffolk coastal landscape. This was an interpretation Eno acknowledged might have been inaccurate, as he doubted the veracity of his memory.

Eno was concerned with the emotions prompted by memory, principally melancholy, a state in which he felt comforted by and associated with the Suffolk coast, rather than the accuracy of the memories themselves. Nor was he prepared to romanticise the English countryside as an idyll.

In a 1982 interview he gave to promote *On Land* he was far from sanguine about rural life:

> When you're out in the country you hear sounds that seem quite lovely and pastoral, but those too are probably the sounds of emergency. That little bird singing is probably sounding some kind of alarm.

The producer built a fully sound-proofed studio, eleven by twelve feet, in his SoHo loft and talked of entering a 'sort of sacred space' as he began his working day in this sealed and controllable environment. Here, in this room that overlooked Broadway, Eno re-imagined the atmosphere of rural isolation he had experienced in East Anglia as a child, and as his eyes cast over the flickering monitors in his studio he created an aural equivalent to the Suffolk gloaming. He would regularly adjust and alter the lighting in his workspace and listen again to the pieces either in a diffused light or in darkness, as though by abnegating the temporal world he allowed himself a more direct route to the subconscious he was dredging for the record's inspiration.

During the recording Eno manipulated found sounds, such as the rattling of discarded metal or wind noise, to create transient and uncertain undertones.

'Lantern Marsh' is one of the album's more overwhelming pieces and is named after the marshland growing around Orford Ness, the twelve or so miles of shingle near

Aldeburgh whose saltings are dashed by the unforgiving waves of the North Sea. The lanterns of the marsh were combustible gases rising from its mire that produced glowing wisps of light that terrified its inhabitants, and occasionally led them to their death as their attempts to grasp their luminescence led them into the quickening mud pools. 'Lantern Marsh' begins with an ominous cry one might associate with wildfowl. These bird cries, and the listener, are then subsumed by an unnerving sound that produces a sense of electric horror.

The baleful presence of the lanterns had long been a source of trepidation. In the seventh century St Botolph decreed that the malodorous swamps around the Ness at Iken be drained in order to expel devils.

Orford Ness was commandeered by the Royal Flying Corps during the First World War then used by the RAF until the late 1950s, when the area was permanently sealed off from the public. A decade later a network of hangars, bunkers and strange, pagoda-like edifices and rows of gaunt fan pylons were constructed on the shingle as the Ness became the headquarters for Cobra Mist, a backscatter radar system developed to detect signals of an incipient nuclear attack. The system had faults, unknown frequencies regularly interrupted the surveillance equipment with indistinct noise and the station was disbanded in 1972.

On the coast 140 miles south of Orford Ness is Dungeness power station, a more visible nuclear building standing on shingle, in sight of which Derek Jarman, when not working in London or in the city for hospital visits, lived at Prospect Cottage, a former fisherman's lodge.

The final film to bear Jarman's name was the posthumously released *Glitterbug* a collage of Super 8 footage that begins in the director's early twenties when he lived in a warehouse on the wharf at Shad Thames. There, in what was unusual accommodation for the time, he had installed a greenhouse in which to sleep. A few seconds of footage of this glass bedroom and other details from this part of his life that he detailed in *Dancing Ledge*, his first volume of journals, appear on screen during *Glitterbug*.

Other moments from the ensuing decades, footage of friends, lovers and collaborators are cut together to form a remarkable self-portrait. The soundtrack that accompanies this footage with which it shares a discordant beauty is by Eno.

In *Modern Nature,* the volume of his journals that cover his life at Prospect Cottage, *Ambient 4: On Land* is one of the few pieces of non-classical music Jarman notes listening to:

28 August.

Eno's *On Land* is the music of my view; a crescent moon under a dog star, clouds scudding in the grey dawn.
I tidied the wood from the back of the house and spent the afternoon picking blackberries for jam. Noticed very

few butterflies at the Long Pits, which have almost dried up; but a host of large dragonflies. The blackberries are just ripening and cascade across the light green bushes, blood-red like raw meat. It was hard work and I got torn to bits.

In another entry Jarman writes of his admiration for the young author Denton Welch who wrote of the English countryside during the war years:

10 February.

Finished my breakfast on the sofa, covered by my grandmother's old travelling rug I read Denton Welch's memoirs. Crystalline descriptions and acute observations. I wish writing came naturally to me.

On first reading these lines I was struck by the symmetry of one writer of a journal commending another. When I finally came across a copy of Welch's out-of-print journals I was similarly struck by a passage that might equally have been written by Jarman to describe his surroundings (although the landscape Welch describes differs from that of Prospect Cottage):

15 June.

Raining, aeroplane droning, trees soughing,

I am lying in bed now, so I imagine, as I have imagined

how many times before, a stone cottage on some heath or moor. A cottage that is reached by a footpath winding through wet grass and heather, bracken, harebell, thistles.

This evocation derives from a sense of the English landscape that includes the gardens where Virginia Astley imagined we might feel secure, the coastline of Brian Eno's Suffolk childhood, and Prospect Cottage and its garden created by Jarman's visionary imagination.

During the period when I was listening to *Deux Filles*, I visited the cinema to see *Blue*, the last film to be released by Jarman when alive, and noted from the poster that the film's music was composed by Simon Fisher Turner.

As the film progresses the audience's eyes learn to focus and focus again at the expanse of ultramarine monochrome that appears to float on the screen. While watching *Blue* I thought for a time I was staring at a river, and imagined a current and began to determine its strength. This must have been a common experience for those watching and as the film progressed a hesitant but noticeable empathy developed between those of us present, as though together we were learning to see in a particular way for the first time.

In quiet passages of the soundtrack I recognised a tone in Fisher Turner's contemplative score and heard again the circulation of air hover like a breath over every note. In these reflective moments, when the richness of Jarman's voice enhanced the poignancy of the memories he described,

I was reminded of an entry in *Modern Nature*, the book of journals he wrote while resident at Prospect Cottage.

He describes the intensity of the heat and languorous haze in which he finds himself drifting through a late summer's day. At one point Jarman has achieved such a becalmed state that by some form of alchemy he appears to have altered time to his preferred pace. He is aware of little else other than the sound of seed heads cracking in the sunlight and scattering their contents on the pebbles below.

This serenity is all the more powerful for being interrupted by the pain and suffering evident in other passages in *Blue*.

Inspired by the soundtrack to *Blue* I determined to play *On Land* the following day in Revolver. A photocopy of an essay Eno had written to accompany the release had been inserted in the second-hand copy I found.

We feel affinities not only with the past, but also with the futures that didn't materialize, and with the other variations of the present that we suspect run parallel to the one we have agreed to live in.

As I read this sentence I was reminded again of 'Burnt Norton':

Time past and time future
Allow but a little consciousness.
To be conscious is not to be in time

But only in time can the moment in the rose-garden,
The moment in the arbour where the rain beat,
The moment in the draughty church at smokefall
Be remembered; involved with past and future.
Only through time time is conquered.

The pastoral is inseparable from memory, as is the air circulating the subdued note played in isolation that, in the words of Jarman describing the effect of watching *Blue*, 'transcends the solemn geography of human limits'.

5

The records that matched the sleeves on display in the racks were stored in wooden shelves behind the counter and filed either in numerical or in alphabetical order, according to catalogue number. Every record for sale was housed in a sleeve known as a master bag. When they arrived at the shop from the suppliers, master bags were white, pristine card that usually had a circle cut out in the middle so the label could be seen, although I can recall seeing a new master bag in Revolver only rarely.

Nearly all our master bags that were in use had been repaired and recycled. The corners had usually been stuck with address labels that had been applied to conceal the original catalogue numbers and create a new surface to write on. Any bags with split seams were similarly mended with masking tape. After years of handling and of absorbing dust in the filing system, many of the master bags had developed a patina similar to the yellowing endpapers of a frequently borrowed library book. Their perpetual use invited a form of carbon dating, as tracing and inspecting the titles and number of copies sold written on a single master bag provided a snapshot of Revolver's sales history.

When a delivery of new releases required filing, I had developed a habit of looking for evidence of a past life in any master bag I chose from the pile stacked arbitrarily in the back room. I would scan the letters and numbers on a bag with disbelief at the number of copies and subsequent reorders sold. Inevitably my surprise was followed by a short bout of melancholy at seeing written evidence that the days of the shop as a force in record-selling were now past.

One grey Bristol afternoon I was going through the mound in the back room and came across a dilapidated master bag that, with a little repair, would once again become functional. Its seams had been reinforced by masking tape placed in layers over strips of Sellotape that age had turned dark and brittle. The cardboard had developed a rich sheen from over fifteen years use. Both its sides had countless catalogue numbers from previous releases. In one corner was a detailed set of markings including the title of the record written in naïf block capitals:

'EDEN'.

Underneath, the catalogue number:

'Blanco GB: BYN 2'

The artist's name 'Everything But The Girl' had been rendered in a semi-acronym:

'Everything BTG'

The date of the album's release had been included with its title:

(March '84)

and was accompanied by a number written in a dashed-off scrawl:

(100)

I easily grew wistful at the number of records Revolver had once been capable of selling and was unsurprised that it had initially ordered a hundred copies of the debut Everything But The Girl album. What I found more distracting were the dates and figures that had been written underneath the original inscription. In different-coloured inks and changing handwriting was a series of numbers which extended over a three- or four-year period:

(30) (20) (15) (20) (10)

I scanned the column of figures and realised that Revolver had continued to order *Eden* in significant quantities years after its release, to such an extent that for the duration of the title's availability on vinyl, the shop must have sold almost a thousand copies.

The record for which I was recycling the *Eden* master bag was unlikely to sell more than a handful. Mainly this was due to its being a semi-legitimate release that had been manufactured in a limited thousand-copy run. The album, *Space Is the Place* by Sun Ra, had originally been released in 1974. The bootleg copy I was filing was made with care and attentiveness. It came in a gatefold sleeve that was a reasonable facsimile of the original, although the cardboard itself was somewhat flimsy and the lines taken from Sun Ra's book of poetry, *The Immeasurable Equation*, printed on one side of the inside sleeve were difficult to read. The vinyl pressing was also a little flat and compressed, but such was the demand for records by Sun Ra in Revolver we were certain to sell the scant few copies we had managed to order.

A visit from a customer interrupted my filing. They had brought to the counter *Protection* by Massive Attack, an album we sold in significant numbers; enough for me to know the catalogue number by heart and my hands instinctively knew where to reach to locate the vinyl.

The title track of the album and another song, 'Better Things', were co-written and sung by Tracey Thorn of Everything But The Girl. The copies of *Eden* that had sold consistently for years were sold and bought in a shop dominant in steering the city's musical culture. It was gratifying and even surprising to sell the vinyl version of

'Protection' in Revolver even if such transactions felt atypical.

Once the copy of 'Protection' had been sold the shop fell empty and I resumed filing *Space Is The Place*.

As a customer I had often asked Roger about the availability of Sun Ra vinyl. His name was mentioned in interviews in music newspapers and magazines, although frequently more in admiration for his ideas about astrological and planetary identity, it seemed, than for his music.

In 1989 the Blast First label had released *Out There a Minute*, a compilation of Sun Ra recordings from the late 1960s. The few biographical details I had learned about Sun Ra and the Arkestra alluded to their leader's insistence that he hailed from Saturn and the band's capacity to alternate between big band swing pieces and exploratory improvisations. The photographs on *Out There a Minute* showed Sun Ra robed and surrounded by spherical objects and drawings suggestive of ritual. As it was the only Sun Ra record available in Revolver I bought it at first sight.

If I had a lingering sense that I had not fully understood *Out There a Minute*, I enjoyed listening to the album enough to ask Roger if he had additional Sun Ra titles he might sell.

On a rainy weekday morning when we had the shop to ourselves Roger briskly placed a pile of thirty or so records on the counter.

'I might sell you one or two of these,' he said, as he sifted through the albums, 'but they will cost you a bit.'

I had little sense of which record or records to choose. In the middle of the hoard was a particularly handsome gatefold album. On the cover Sun Ra, in a headpiece of gilded metallic wire, was seated at a keyboard in concentrated dignity with his right arm raised as if in an act of benediction. Inside the gatefold were detailed sleeve notes printed in French over a photograph of members of the Arkestra seated during performance. The record was particularly heavy. I noticed that it had been made in France and released on Shandar, a label I assumed to be based there.

At the top of the sleeve were the words 'Sun Ra Nuits de la Fondation Maeght Vol: 1'. Increasingly certain that I would attempt to purchase this exotic record, the title convinced me. As a child I had been transfixed by the elongated, neurotic Giacometti figures, whose presence had a shared similarity to the ash-preserved bodies of Pompeii, as they stood against the azure Mediterranean sky of the Fondation Maeght in St Paul de Vence. The realisation that Sun Ra and the Arkestra had played on a stage built in the centre of modern art's courtyard during a starlit evening in Provence was a beguiling proposition.

Memories of childhood holidays in the South of France remained unspoken as I began my negotiations with Roger. I decided he might infer that foreign vacations indicated wealth and might include these assumptions in the price. (This proved prescient. Years later, a friend recounted that, while in Bristol for a weekend, he had persuaded Roger that his love of free jazz was genuine and they had embarked on a transaction over rare Albert Ayler records. The original offer was rescinded and the price increased once my friend had, perhaps naively, produced a Coutts & Co. chequebook.)

'This one will cost you a tenner' said Roger.

Although I could little afford further purchases, I sensed that this opportunity might not arise again and spent a moment lingering over the pile in front of Roger. Another record caught my attention. Once more it was the name of the record label that I had found intriguing.

'This one was released on Y?' I asked Roger. 'Was that . . .'

'Y,' he smiled back. 'The Pop Group's label.'

The members of the Pop Group had met while at school in Bristol in the mid-1970s. The band's guitarist and drummer, Gareth Sager and Bruce Smith, were pupils at Cotham Grammar School, and singer Mark Stewart attended Bristol Grammar School. Both schools were within a short walk of Revolver as was another school, Clifton College. The shop was attractive to pupils wishing to avoid classes and the long corridor was considered a place where cigarettes could be smoked unhindered while in school uniform.

Revolver's then owner Chris Parker had a benign attitude towards playing records for anyone loitering in the shop, particularly if they lacked the means to make purchases. Stewart, Sager, Smith and their contemporaries were inquisitive enough to ask to hear the music of Ornette Coleman, Don Cherry and Roland Kirk and received in Revolver an alternative education to their school syllabus.

The sister of Mark Springer, a friend of Stewart, Sager and Smith who would join the latter two as pianist in the band Rip, Rig + Panic, had long-standing connections with the organisers of blues parties and sound systems in St Paul's. Stewart's grandparents also lived in the area, which meant that as teenagers the future members of the Pop Group experienced dub in its natural context. Visiting sound systems such as Metro Media from Jamaica and Stereograph, a London system that was often hosted at Bristol, left their mark on Stewart as well as the city's resident systems such as Enterprise.

Such was their affinity and enjoyment of the sound systems, Stewart and Sager made a point of visiting Revolver on the days that the shop took delivery of 'pre's and dubplates, and stood beside the sound-system operators as they listened to the new releases.

As a result, and despite the fact they were under age, the Pop Group were admitted to the Dug Out, a club on Park Row a few hundred yards from Revolver. The Dug Out became identified with the city's love of compounding and mixing different styles of music to create an inclusive, free form, genre synonymous with Bristol.

The Pop Group's experience of the Dug Out, the St Paul's sound systems and of hearing free jazz played in Revolver was audible in their first recordings made with the delirium of youth. Their debut album 'Y' (the letter that had also given name to their record label) was disorientated and stretched by Dub's transmutation of musical structure. Dennis Bovell who, while running his own Jah Sufferer sound system frequently distressed the frequencies of the pre-amps until they bled, produced the record. His willingness to distort and manipulate sound rather than merely record it ensured his position as the country's most respected artist/producer in the reggae industry, and made him especially receptive to the Pop Group's ideas and experiments.

The millenarian outlook on 'Y' was similar in theme to the two Sun Ra records released on the Pop Group's label, an album *Strange Celestial Road*, the record Roger sold to me, and a 12" EP called *Nuclear War*.

'I'll Wait For You', the third song on 'Strange Celestial Road', was sung by June Tyson, Rhoda Blount and other members of the Arkestra and imagines an unknown, cosmic hinterland:

> In some far off place
> Many light years in space
> I'll wait for you
> Where human feet have never trod
> I'll wait for you
> Where human eyes have never seen
> I'll wait for you

I'll build a world of abstract dreams
And wait for you

'Nuclear War' is a more despairing song. Sun Ra half
sings and half intones his concerns over two repeated
piano chords played in a soft rolling pattern. Ra is
accompanied by June Tyson and Tyrone Hill of the
Arkestra, who participate in a call and response with
their leader over the loose drum rhythm set down by Eric
'Samarai Celestial' Walker.

Nuclear War
Talking about
Nuclear War
It's a Motherfucker
Don't you know
If they push that button
Your ass gotta go
They're talking about
This nuclear war
You can kiss your ass goodbye . . .
Gonna blast your ass
So high in the sky
Radiation
Mutation
Fire
Hydrogen bombs

Atomic bombs
What you gonna do?
Without yo ass?
Fire
Melting
People
Buildings
Burnt grass

There was a further stock of Sun Ra albums in Revolver that Roger had neglected to show me as a customer and that I would be permitted to see only as a member of staff. The records carried no information. The sleeves consisted solely of stiff plain white cardboard decorated with minimal but colourful felt-tip lines. The vinyl itself lacked printed labels, instead a gloss plastic circle remained uncovered at their centre.

I learnt that these were records that had been privately pressed by Sun Ra and the Arkestra themselves. In my romantic imagination I assumed that Revolver had acquired them through the shop's affiliation with Y records and Rough Trade and that Sun Ra had passed on a box of records to the Pop Group in recognition of kindred souls. I envisaged a dialogue between Mark Stewart and Sun Ra during which Ra elucidated his cosmic ancestry. Although I later learned that this conversation had indeed taken place, the meeting had not been held in Revolver.

I was unable to identify the provenance of the innominate Sun Ra records with any certainty. I was informed they were genuine and had probably been held by Ra or, more likely, by Marshall Allen or John Gilmore of the Arkestra, but the means by which they had reached Revolver was never known.

The Y label was operational for only a few years and was run from an office in London by Dick O'Dell, the manager of the Pop Group who for a short period also managed the Slits. Although their music lacked the feverishness of the Pop Group, Y released music by Bristol bands that shared a similar capricious and volatile energy. Pigbag, whom Roger had known in Cheltenham, played compelling brass-led instrumentals that were commercially successful. Another Y act, Maximum Joy, sounded equally spirited if less immediately approachable. The B side of Maximum Joy's first single released in 1981 was titled 'Silent Street/Silent Dub', a phrase that evokes the experience of walking through Bristol between the twilight and the dawn. Maximum Joy released their final record two years later, a cover version of 'Why Can't We Live Together'.

To accompany their last single Maximum Joy issued a 12" remix. The track featured backing vocals from its producer, Dennis Bovell, and Paul 'Nelly' Hooper, who had recently joined the band and was credited with playing Syndrums.

There had been a vibrancy to much of the music released on Y that overshadowed the occasional missed notes or hurried song-ending that created a sense of urgency, a sense that had doubtless felt infectious and stimulating to their audience. The final Maximum Joy release was a break with this sensibility. The remix had been constructed and edited precisely at Studio 80, Dennis Bovell's state of the art recording facility and featured a breakbeat functioning as the lead instrument.

A year after 'Why Can't We Live Together' was released Hooper would no longer be 'Nelly' but 'Nellee', a founding member of the Wild Bunch, a new and impulsive Bristol sound system whose members included the six-and-a-half-foot tall Grantley Marshall from Long Ashton, a DJ with a residency at the Dug Out who also worked in Revolver by day.

When the Pop Group had played concerts in Bristol, notably at the Trinity Centre, a converted church in Lawrence Hill that regularly hosted sound systems, Marshall's DJ sets featured selections from his reggae and dub collection and had created the appropriate atmosphere before the band took the stage. The Pop Group were filmed at one of their Trinity performances for the video that accompanied their debut single 'She Is Beyond Good and Evil'. I had watched a static-saturated VHS copy. The band's on-stage convulsions were mesmerising and the dancing crowd had a similar self-willed energy that was in marked contrast to concerts in the city I attended, or later promoted, that invariably attracted an audience happy to be seated on the floor.

I understood some years later that the Pop Group had harnessed a particular vitality rarely present at concerts by guitar bands. Their performances of 'We Are Time' and 'Thief of Fire' were essentially deconstructions of the songs, transforming them either into minimal bass-and-drum dance patterns or allowing them to disintegrate into a chaos of echo, melodica and screams that had the intensity of an exorcism.

For his Wednesday night residency at the Dug Out, Marshall, now known as Daddy G, included import copies of the first electro and hip-hop singles in his sets to mix with selections from his expansive dub collection. A friend, Miles Johnson, whom Marshall had met through a shared love of punk concerts and who played records as DJ Milo, joined Hooper and Marshall in the embryonic Wild Bunch. Another associate, Claude Williams, would stand behind the system's decks to rap over their selections as Willy Wee, and trade rhymes with Robert Del Naja, a young local graffiti artist with a national reputation and the tag 3D.

In time the Wild Bunch would gain affiliate members and associates. A young hip-hop fan named Andrew Vowles temporarily blind-sided Marshall at the Revolver counter with a request for an obscure import 12" with which he was unfamiliar. Marshall had noticed Vowles at Dug Out sessions and suggested Vowles shared his knowledge of esoteric tracks with the sound system and joined the Wild Bunch as 'Mushroom', a name inspired by a video game.

*

When I arrived in Bristol, the Dug Out had been closed for over two years, although the club was often referred to in op-ed pieces about licensing and nightlife in *Venue*. I had read that the members of the Wild Bunch were pursuing solo projects and often saw mention of a local production duo called Smith and Mighty, although it was hard to determine whether their music had been released or made available. A pub near the house where I lived when I first moved to the city called the Montpelier Hotel had an upstairs pool room with a jukebox that contained, I later realised, many of the songs that had been popular in the Dug Out. Along the walls of the pool room was a series of graffiti paintings and stencils that had a reoccurring, pop-art quality recognisable from similar artwork on the walls of Bristol streets. Although too self-conscious to enquire of their origin, some months after first visiting the pub I noticed '3D' sprayed in the bottom right-hand corner of the paintings.

In a photograph taken of the Wild Bunch at the Dug Out, several of the band's faces are locked in concentration, as though the members of the sound system are all staring at one another in anticipation of who might be the first to appropriate the turntable. They cluster around the record decks in a manner that suggests the DJ booth is struggling to contain their ideas as well as their bodies.

Marshall's height made him look similarly confined underneath the low Revolver ceiling. The shop had recently installed a secondary set of speakers at the far end of the room near the doorway, which had been covered with handfuls of Wild Bunch stickers.

On Fridays many of the sound-system operators who arrived at the shop to listen to 'pre's and dubplates would arrange to meet later in the evening at the Dug Out. It was later explained to me by Marshall that the shop and the club were two of the few reasons for many of his neighbours to leave St Paul's to journey on foot up into Clifton.

The Wild Bunch's reputation as a sound system that ran exuberant and inclusive nights in a New York B-boy style grew from their residency at the Dug Out. The parties they hosted on the corner of Campbell Street where Marshall and Johnson lived, or outdoors on the Downs, or the impromptu late-night listening sessions they encouraged and participated in around the stereos of friends all felt communal to those present

Other resident sound systems such as 2Bad proved equally popular at the Dug Out, where break dancing was encouraged on the downstairs dance floor. The Wild Bunch held an advantage over their contemporaries, however, as at Revolver Marshall had access to a weekly supply of new music. He would regularly neglect to inform other sound-system operators of a particularly notable release; instead he added any copy he had been able to source to his personal tab. The competitive nature of the Wild Bunch was marked. Vowles would tear the labels from recent import 12" singles so their content remained unknown and could not be identified or 'bitten' by other systems. Similarly Milo and Hooper would go as far as gluing a 7" on to a 12" to confuse any onlookers who would struggle to identify which format was playing in the half-light of the downstairs room of the Dug Out.

For the Wild Bunch Bristol and New York were their twin points of cultural orientation. The sense that London felt like an irrelevance was reinforced by their battles with the capital's sound systems whose scope and attitude they considered limited by musical fashions and conservatism. These encounters only served to encourage their quiet, unassuming, particularly Bristolian self-confidence.

Such boasts were qualified by the release of the debut Wild Bunch single 'Tearin' down the Avenue' on Fourth & Broadway in 1986. As the record company gave the single an American-only release, 'Tearin' down the Avenue' is a record few have ever seen or heard. This was perhaps an attempt at ensuring the 12" was treated as a white label to be distributed solely among DJs. More confusingly, there are those who believe, or perhaps fantasise, that the Wild Bunch had signed an American-only deal for one record.

What is certain is that at its time of release 'Tearin' down the Avenue' seemed unobtainable, and the mystery that surrounded the release added to the sense that the Wild Bunch were as much an enigma as they were a sound system.

An early version of the song was played on the DJ Tim Westwood's show on the pirate radio station LWR. It featured an introductory verse from 3D containing the line 'welcome together around this Massive Attack'.

A year later the Wild Bunch's affinity with hip-hop was authenticated when the group were asked to remix 'Move the Crowd' by Eric B & Rakim. A second Wild Bunch single on Fourth & Broadway, 'Friends and Countrymen', was given a wider release than their debut. Photo shoots and notices in the style magazines accompanied the record in which the members of the sound system came across as simultaneously iconoclastic and reticent. It was the single's B side, 'The Look of Love', an affecting cover version sung by the vocalist Shara Nelson and produced by Smith and Mighty, that drew most attention.

There was one final appearance by the Wild Bunch recorded on vinyl.

Morgan McVey, a duo signed to Stock Aitken Waterman's label SAW, released a solitary 12" titled 'Looking Good Diving'. The record's B side, 'Diving with the Wild Bunch', was a remix that featured Cameron McVey's partner Neneh Cherry. As a former member of Rip, Rig + Panic, Cherry was friendly and familiar to the Bristol musicians.

'Looking Good Diving' and 'Diving with the Wild Bunch' was constructed around a forthright and exhilarating rap by Cherry and formed the basis of her debut single 'Buffalo Stance'.

On New Year's Eve 1987 the Wild Bunch hosted a party at the Crypt on Ashley Road in St Paul's that featured a sound clash between themselves and London's Soul II Soul, the London sound system that Nellee Hooper would soon join and whose debut album he would produce. The evening was one of the final Wild Bunch parties of note in Bristol. There would be no official ending to their career, particularly as 'career' was a misnomer for their activities and the experiences they created.

The Wild Bunch had existed as a sound system that toured internationally as far as Japan and flourished in their home city during an era of community policing. The unlicensed parties they hosted on the Downs, or at such makeshift venues as the Red House Warehouse in St Paul's or the disused Volkswagen Centre nearby, had been celebratory, pioneering evenings that passed off without incident. Instead of being terminated by the authorities and having their equipment confiscated or destroyed, as had happened to their forebears, the Wild Bunch had been allowed a freedom of expression in which a new form of urban hedonism was allowed to flourish, as the bass lines ran until dawn or to whenever they had reached their natural conclusion.

As the Wild Bunch gradually ceased to function, several of their contemporaries released their first recordings in 1988. Smith and Mighty started the label Three Stripe in order to release their productions of Bacharach and David compositions reinterpreted as break-beat torch songs. The duo also recorded an evocative cover version of Rose Royce's 'Wishing on a Star' by Fresh Four, a young DJ crew who achieved a Top 20 chart position.

The Three Stripe label had been partly financed by Lloyd Harris and Mike Chadwick in Revolver. They were in the process of selling the shop as a going concern to Roger. Harris and Chadwick had plans to grow their distribution company and had taken over a warehouse on Dove Lane in St Paul's. The fact the shop and the distributor shared a common name understandably confused people and was an occasional source of tension.

With reasonable amiability the Wild Bunch fragmented and dispersed, Nellee Hooper moved to London and Milo Johnson emigrated to New York City. Daddy G, 3D and Mushroom took the name Massive Attack with the intention of producing a collaborative album. Their plans for the record included contributions from floating affiliate members including Horace Andy, Shara Nelson, Willy Wee and Tricky Kid, a rapper and member of the Wild Bunch entourage during its final days.

The first Massive Attack single 'Any Love' was released on Massive Attack Records in 1989 and credited to Daddy

G and Carlton alone. The lead track was a cover version of a Chaka Khan song and featured the ethereal voice of Carlton, a Bristolian singer who had previously worked with the track's producers Smith and Mighty.

The Revolver logo is printed on the information sticker placed on the cover of the 12", together with the record's credits, as Harris and Chadwick had similarly financed and distributed the single's release.

In the same year Revolver Distribution had also entered into an agreement with Heavenly, a London-based label established by Jeff Barrett, an alumnus of the shop. Barrett had been first approached by Harris to manage Revolver while working as the independent label buyer at HMV in Plymouth, and moved to Bristol to work behind the counter for a year between 1983 and 1984. The arrangement between Heavenly and Revolver was short-lived and lasted little more than twelve months, during which Heavenly achieved chart positions for two of its first signings, Flowered Up and St Etienne.

*

In early 1990 the Arnolfini gallery on the Bristol Quays staged an exhibition of new work by Richard Long. Although Long had been established as one of the significant artists of his generation for many years, there was an added frisson to the Arnolfini exhibition. Long was a life-long Bristol resident and his installations and wall paintings included local materials such as River Avon mud and slate gathered from the banks of the Severn.

The pieces on display were large scale. One sculpture, a circular composition of rocks filled the entire ground-floor gallery. The overall tone of the installation was contemplative. There were gradations in the colour of the slate that were discernible against the white gallery walls. In their natural surroundings these subtle differences may have been harder to notice, as on a grey day looking out in the sea light where the shoreline, rocks and sky have merged into an indeterminate and darkening presence on the horizon. When considered individually under the bright gallery lights the colour palette contained in each rock appeared celestial.

In another room Long had created one of his signature tonal compositions, a mud painting, that ran along the length of a wall. The lines were made with repetitive, circular strokes whose varying degrees of thickness created the sense of an infinite pattern that had stalled. As if a wave had fallen against the gallery wall and in doing so had damaged its memory and forgotten how to recede.

In the final room were hung some of the artist's works on paper that were mainly short prose poems that gave details of completed walks. Long would sometimes include two or three word phrases from his journey suggestive of psychological reflection. At other times he presented a factual representation of his route.

One piece, 'White Light Walk', described a walk that had taken place near Bristol three years earlier:

WHITE LIGHT WALK

RED LEAVES ON A JAPANESE MAPLE
ORANGE SUN AT 4 MILES
YELLOW PARSNIPS AT 23 MILES
GREEN RIVER SLIME AT 45 MILES
BLUE EYES OF A CHILD AT 56 MILES
INDIGO JUICE OF A BLACKBERRY AT 69 MILES
VIOLET WILD CYCLAMEN AT 72 MILES

AVON, ENGLAND 1987

'Two Sahara Stones' from the following year described a stationary action that required a similar level of energy and concentration to complete a long walk:

TWO SAHARA STONES

SITTING ON A MOUNTAIN TOP
IN THE HOGGAR
CLAPPING TWO FLAT STONES TOGETHER
A THOUSAND TIMES

1988

For this exhibition at Arnolfini, Long had not written any supporting material. In *Words after the Fact*, a booklet published to accompany his previous show at the gallery in 1983, he had however described his methods:

> The freedom to use precisely all degrees of visibility
> and permanence is important in my work. Art can be
> a step or a stone. A sculpture, a map, a text, a
>   photograph;
> all the forms of my work are equal and complementary.
> The knowledge of my actions, in whatever form,
> is the art. My art is the essence of my experience,
> not a representation of it.

*

As plans were finalised for the release of their debut album *Blue Lines*, Massive Attack were informed by their record company that their name had to undergo a temporary abbreviation. The Gulf War was under way and placing the words 'massive' and 'attack' together was considered incendiary and provocative. On the promotional posters for the record, *Blue Lines* was credited to 'Massive'. In Bristol this change felt apposite, as it was by this one word that the band were known colloquially in the city. The posters featured 3D's graffiti, which I recognised from the pool room in the Montpelier Hotel. They included small insignia against which were written 'Wild Bunch Recording' and another phrase, 'Original Chief Rockers', that the group had once considered using as a name.

In Bristol cassette copies of *Blue Lines* were circulating some time before the album's release. In effect Massive Attack had bootlegged themselves and made a gift of the music to those who had supported and encouraged them and to those as well, who had blown or merely worn their whistles and danced at their parties.

At the time of its release I furtively asked in Revolver if a listening copy of *Blue Lines* was available. I was little more than a loyal and inquisitive customer but was told that I could borrow the tape held behind the counter if I returned it within a few days. I explained that I lacked the facilities to duplicate a cassette, but my attempt at reassurance was waived away with an accompanying smile as I was handed an unmarked tape. The cassette contained no information other than a tick written on a generic label applied to its A side.

I left the counter and loitered for a moment in the corridor. I reached for my Walkman and substituted its contents for this new tape that still held the scent of its clean plastic casing.

Once on the pavement I turned right and began walking home in the dusk. As the sound of sibilant wind gave way to the propulsive bass line of 'Safe from Harm' my footsteps fell into a rhythm and I settled into my stride as I walked the length of Park Row. On my right was the former site of the Dug Out. Once the song's first chorus had been completed I passed the bottom of St Michael's Hill where the café Special K, the daytime haunt of the group and many of their associates, had recently closed.

By the time I had reached the Upper Maudlin Street end of Jamaica Street, drizzle had settled in small patches on my face. The street always felt liminal, as though it were a natural border between the aspirational commerce of Clifton, the clothes and record shops, the cafés and restaurants, and the less ostentatious, soft-focus source of much of the city's creativity that was located past the border of Stokes Croft and into the heartlands of Montpelier and St Paul's.

The Bell, a pub just off Jamaica Street, was one of the few places where the city's musicians were known to congregate. It abutted a hostel for the homeless and its other neighbouring building was a school for the deaf. Other than a massage parlour there were few other occupied buildings on the other side of Jamaica Street. At one end was a small factory. I had once walked past its gates as a bell rang across its yard and staff filed together towards a canteen for lunch. A row of empty buildings with boarded-up windows and doors occupied the street's middle section. I had occasionally heard bands rehearse in a basement that I assumed belonged to one of these properties.

At the junction with Stokes Croft was a taller building

where I knew warehouse parties had recently been held on its second and third floors. On a weekday morning under a grey sky, Jamaica Street and Stokes Croft felt uneventful and moribund. Experienced at night, particularly when looking out from windows of the elevated buildings nearby, the area had a sodium glow that illuminated the languid circulation of energy below that spread out gradually across the city.

There was a further aspect to Bristol's civic character, one that was understood but remained unarticulated. I was a temporary resident, but I had lived in the city for four years and realised that the past inhabited its atmosphere in a manner that was rarely popular or agreed upon, as a satisfactory settlement that recognised and confronted its slave-trading heritage had yet to be proposed. And if the city ever felt segregated, to walk east along Jamaica Street was to walk along a bloodline that reflected Bristol's late twentieth-century heterogeneous identity.

I turned on to Stokes Croft and the wind picked up slightly, as it always seemed to at that corner. As I listened to 'Be Thankful For What You've Got' I paused for a moment then rewound the tape. A section in the song where the organ part is suddenly scratched, as if on a turntable, had temporarily thrown me and I listened to this passage again in order to check my Walkman had not malfunctioned. I had allowed the tape to penetrate my subconscious during this rainy walk. A tendency of mine to evaluate a piece of music on first hearing was developing into a personal fault. The need to concentrate on traffic, road crossings and fellow pedestrians had temporarily negated this habit and ensured I listened to these songs in a sensory rather than analytical manner.

My walking half-reverie had led me to the top of Picton Street. 'Five Man Army' began as drums reverberated in a soft echo and minimal, purposeful bass notes created an atmosphere of faint trepidation. I associated the sound with this environment. At this instant, I thought, if I remove my headphones a similar low end frequency would be audible from the stereos of these houses I am passing.

Some moments later as I walked underneath the arch of the Montpelier Hotel I grew receptive to the song's lyrics and for the first time a line from 3D's verse,

This is the miracle of the dub dubplate selection.

Willy Wee, who had exchanged lyrics with 3D in the Wild Bunch, spoke the next line in Bristolian dialect,

So whether you're black or white or half-caste
   in your complexion

The second half of 'Five Man Army', which runs for almost three minutes consisting solely of Horace Andy's lachrymose vocal scats, the backing rhythm track and a vaporous dub, a Bristol form of dub, that drifted across the steep streets and sturdy scruffy houses, faded slowly to silence. I was now home. The walk, one I undertook at least twice a day had begun in Clifton and finished in Montpelier.

Significant locations involved in the creation of *Blue Lines* were absent from my journey. The route had not included any of the recording studios used. These were Neneh Cherry's house in London, where much of the sampling for the album had been done, Matrix Studio where the album's producer Johnny Dollar had sequenced the tapes and Coach House Studios in Clifton, a former BBC studio located in a quiet Georgian side street within sight of the suspension bridge.

BLUE LINES
REVOLVER TO THE DUG OUT
SAFE FROM HARM
SPECIAL K'S TO JAMAICA STREET
BE THANKFUL FOR WHAT YOU'VE GOT
STOKES CROFT AND THE JUNCTION OF PICTON STREET
   AND ASHLEY ROAD LEADING TO CAMPBELL STREET
   TO THE MONTPELIER HOTEL
FIVE MAN ARMY

It was far from definitive in its prescription, but to some extent, while listening to the album for the first time, I had subconsciously undertaken my own equivalent of an elemental Richard Long walk in discovery of *Blue Lines*.

6

Skigersta is one of the sixteen or so settlements that comprise the community of Ness on the Isle of Lewis, the northernmost point of the Outer Hebrides. The area's principal landmark is the Butt of Lewis, a lighthouse at the far tip of the island that is racked in all weathers by the remorseless North Atlantic waves. Throughout the Hebrides the Sabbath is observed with an inalterable stringency. The ferries to the mainland lie moored on a Sunday and the islands' shops remain closed throughout the day. The sense of fixed traditions is reinforced by the long-upheld right of many of the islanders to gather peat for use as fuel, dark stacks of which can be seen drying across the moors.

A small coastal fishing village, Skigersta extends for no more than a mile along the western shore of Lewis. Remnants of fish-curing bothies still stand near the beach and across the expanse of moorland that surrounds Skigersta are the ruins of sheilings, the temporary dwellings in which farmers would sleep while their sheep graze on common land during the summer. As one gazes out to sea the offing is as hard to determine as on any archipelago, but perhaps here in the far north such boundaries have long disintegrated. Along one of the peat tracks that lead inland away from the shore is a small group of buildings that was once used as a chicken farm.

The sheds and outhouses are well maintained; their interiors are lined with rows of wooden shelves and the floor is dense with packing cases. Its current owners use the chicken sheds for an activity that is even more precarious than the subsistence farming of poultry.

Here at one of the edges of the world are the international headquarters of Impetus Distribution, the holding point and clearing house of a distinct and ornery music and philosophy: British avant-garde free jazz and improvisation.

Impetus was founded by two bearded young men, Kenneth Ansell and Paul Acott-Stephens, in the late 1970s. Initially the company traded as a record label. The first release on Impetus Records was *Wipe Out*, a four-vinyl-LP box set of a live recording of Amalgam, a British free jazz group led by the saxophonist Trevor Watts.

In most photographs of Amalgam performances, Watts is wearing glasses and has an unruly head of curly hair. His T-shirts or sweaters further lend him the air of a social sciences lecturer, although the energy with which he appears to be playing his alto saxophone suggests a vitality that could only succeed on its own unconstrained terms. A cursory attempt – of which it is fair to suppose there may have only been a few – at listening to all eight vinyl sides of

Wipe Out confirms such a vitality, but might perhaps put a strain on the listener's own.

*

Trevor Watts took up the saxophone in the Royal Air Force during his National Service where he met and began playing with John Stevens, a student at the RAF School of Music at Uxbridge. Stevens, a mercurial drummer, drinker and tireless organiser, would become a permanent and invigorating presence in British free music until his death aged fifty-four in 1993. Upon leaving the RAF in the mid-1960s Stevens became immersed in Soho's lively hard-bop clubs where he would accompany Stan Tracey, Tubby Hayes and the scene's de facto custodian, Ronnie Scott. Along with trombonist Paul Rutherford, another friend from the RAF, Watts followed a more diffuse musical direction and began leading a quintet that drew on the fast-developing ideas about improvisation then being pioneered by Ornette Coleman in New York. By 1966 Stevens was also convinced and invigorated by the radical possibilities afforded by improv. Together with Watts and Rutherford the newly inspired Stevens founded a group that would make free-form experimentation its *raison d'être* and have a profound, nuanced effect on contemporary music: the Spontaneous Music Ensemble.

Until Stevens's death the Spontaneous Music Ensemble

was a perpetually shifting cell. Stevens was the ensemble's one constant member throughout its existence; he imagined the ensemble as a collective for listening as much as for playing. His only fixed instruction to anyone participating in it was that if they were unable to hear what the other members were playing, then they themselves were playing too loud. This was a philosophy that went beyond the closely self-scrutinised performances of the Spontaneous Music Ensemble. The need to listen to one another carefully, Stevens insisted, was a fundamental human right in constant need of assertion. From its inception the ensemble frequently played to audiences as small as one. The list of the venues in which they performed illustrates the dissipation in energies of the British counter-culture from its high water mark in the late 1960s.

In their early years, when radical ideas were a feature of every creative community in London, the Spontaneous Music Ensemble performed in Arts Labs and small performance spaces in central London. Stevens discovered one such space himself, located up four flights of stairs in a Covent Garden alley, a velvet-draped room called the Little Theatre Club.

Once the house lights had gone up and the actors had departed the theatre at the end of the evening, the Spontaneous Music Ensemble would set up overnight among the stage sets and embark on discursive after-hours sessions that might last uninterrupted until dawn.

A contemporary photograph shows Stevens centre stage at his drum kit, which he has placed underneath a flimsy but charming, hand-painted proscenium arch. His eyes are closed and his wiry frame is suspended over his instruments with great concentration and intensity. High up above Monmouth Street the generation of musicians that would come to define a particular strain of British music: Stevens, Watts, Rutherford, Evan Parker, Maggie Nichols, Derek Bailey, Norma Winstone, John McLaughlin, David Holland and their friends would combine the light-headedness of sleep deprivation with a restless exploratory spirit. The result was a musical form that had never been played before: restrained, challenging yet meditative, a group identity in permanent flux; immersed in this sound world the listeners themselves became members of the Spontaneous Music Ensemble.

The albums that the ensemble recorded were played live in the studio, usually on a single day. Now they exist as rare documents of an understated and intimate music, one that places the significance of silence above the ego and that was played in a spirit of communal listening. On these studio recordings it is possible to hear the musicians develop an idea or phrase that suggests a departure from the group interplay is imminent, only for them to restrain themselves from attempting a solo and to fall back into the selfless playing of the ensemble.

During the late 1970s and into the 1980s the Spontaneous

Music Ensemble would convene for workshops under the glare of the strip-lighting of community centres and classrooms. In its final years shortly before Stevens's death, the ensemble would make sporadic appearances in the reduced circumstances of cramped upstairs rooms in scruffy north London pubs. However small, temporary or uncertain the residency, throughout its lifetime the Spontaneous Music Ensemble would determinedly explore Stevens's tenets of close listening and communal playing.

When he founded the Spontaneous Music Ensemble, Stevens had been influenced by the energy and methods of AMM, an improvising group that had met a year or so earlier. Initially a caucus of three jazz musicians – drummer Eddie Prevost, guitarist Keith Rowe and saxophonist Lou Gare – AMM was convened over a weekend for an exploratory workshop at the Royal College of Art in 1965. The three letters of AMM have, like their members, constantly resisted or, more accurately, negated definition.

The initial AMM workshops produced music that was dense, unruly and formidable. The pieces they improvised were open-ended and might last for over an hour, leaving the musicians physically drained and overwhelmed by the sound they had created.

Such was their notoriety that within a few months of their inception, the composer Cornelius Cardew approached AMM about the possibilities of collaboration.

Unlike the members of AMM or the members of the

Spontaneous Music Ensemble, Cardew's background lay in avant-garde composition rather than jazz. By the time he was interested in working with AMM he had a burgeoning reputation for risk and experimentation along with a disregard for the conventions still prevalent in contemporary composition, especially within the British musical establishment.

After his graduation from the Royal College of Music in the late 1950s, Cardew had spent three years with Karlheinz Stockhausen in his Cologne conservatory, first under his tutelage and then as his assistant. In 1958 Cardew undertook the Darmstadt International Summer Course for New Music and experienced John Cage's revolutionary ideas about indeterminacy, or 'chance' in music at first hand. There he attended a lecture by the American and witnessed the composer give a rare European performance of his *Concert for Piano and Orchestra* with his fellow pianist David Tudor.

Upon his return to Britain in 1960 Cardew began work on the ambitious long-form composition *Treatise* that he named after Wittgenstein's *Tractatus Logico-Philosophicus*, the philosopher's major work that addresses the conceptions of logic and language by suggesting that thoughts and hypotheses are pictures. Its opening proposition is:

The world is everything, that is the case.

The score for *Treatise* is a set of abstract graphic instructions that performers must interpret and adapt as they see fit. As he also occasionally worked as an illustrative designer, Cardew's skills as a draughtsman ensured the score of *Treatise* was an artefact of great visual beauty and the original score took the form of a 134-page cloth-bound book. Its imagery was stimulating and its thick indented pages have the feeling of a divine text. In some passages the symbols in the composition are dense black circles of varying sizes, intersected by right angles. They have the appearance of illustrations in a textbook of advanced astronomy. Elsewhere the score is comprised of innocuous straight lines that suddenly bend and shift into opaque shapes that suggest hieroglyphics, or that mutate into complex matrices of endlessly repeating patterns.

At first glance *Treatise* seems incomprehensible. Cardew reinforces any uncertainty the reader might have by placing a blank stave along the bottom of every page.

The stave suggests formality and structure but lies empty; above it are Cardew's diagrams and enjoinments. Between the blank stave and Cardew's symbols, at some mid-point in the performer and the composer's subconscious, lies the music of *Treatise*.

Musicians who have played *Treatise* often describe the need to resist attempts to decipher Cardew's shapes and images. Instead they assimilate and internalise the composer's drawings and graphic designs until a method of playing the work starts to reveal itself. Without the complete engagement of the musician, *Treatise* remains merely a ravishing sequence of imagery.

In the AMM workshops, Cardew had recognised a freedom and disregard for the conventions of structure along with a willingness to cede control to the animal spirits of improvisation that would allow him to explore and realise his ideas for *Treatise*.

While he worked on his composition, the original trio of AMM, Keith Rowe, Lou Gare and Eddie Prevost, along with Cardew and another musician, the cellist Lawrence Sheaff, recorded an album *AMMMusic* for Elektra Records in June 1966.

The sleeve for *AMMMusic* is striking. It features a yellow-and-white juggernaut rendered in the style of a comic-strip drawing. To the left of the articulated lorry, members of AMM are listed along with their instruments:

Cornelius Cardew: cello, piano, transistor radio
Keith Rowe: guitar, transistor radio
Lawrence Sheaff: cello, clarinet
Lou Gare: saxophone, violin
Eddie Prevost: drums, xylophone

The inclusion of transistor radio in the line-up suggests interference, or the sporadic clouds of white noise a listener experiences while tuning in between signals.

On the reverse sleeve of *AMMMusic* in block capitals is the album's track listing:

SIDE A   LATER DURING A FLAMING RIVIERA SUNSET
SIDE B   AFTER RAPIDLY CIRCLING THE PLAZA

Underneath this text are fifteen photos on a contact sheet of Kodak Safety Film including pictures of the musicians in the studio. They are wearing ties and their hair is cut in short back and sides. Cardew's aquiline features and his air of restless intensity permeate the photographs. Standing together in the seductive environs of a state of the art recording studio, he and the rest of AMM have the studied air of young men alive with the realisation they are creating something unprecedented.

For the recording AMM amplified their instruments with contact microphones which they similarly applied to broken bottles and random household objects. Other images on the contact sheet include a grand piano being prepared and an assemblage of some indeterminate though inauspicious-looking studio equipment.

Alongside the photographs is one long epigrammatic paragraph. The record company had asked AMM for sleeve notes at short notice prior to the release of the album. The musicians hastily agreed to write down a set of aphorisms that they felt reinforced AMM's ethos and anti-identity. (Cardew wasn't present at this meeting.) There are thirteen aphorisms in total. One or two are short almost haiku like:

'Every noise has a note', 'The past always seems intentional, but at the time it appears to be accidental' or 'AMM started itself. It was there a few minutes before we thought of it'.

The most revealing dictum is the longest and most lyrical:

'Playing in AMM sometimes produces a state where you feel sounds in a completely different way from usual. Seeing as if for the first time this reddy-brown object with all the strings going away from the left, a bow going across the strings on the right hand side and interwoven amongst the strings various little things, on top of that plastic lid, and just watch the sound happening.'

'Just watch the sound happening.' These last five words might equally have been an informal direction from Cardew to anyone who might be struggling to interpret the score of *Treatise*.

AMMMusic is a foreboding record during which the listener is immersed in forty minutes of an *art brut* totality. To hear it is a debilitating experience, even in the context of the experimental and progressive spirit of the times of its creation. The recording on *AMMMusic* lies beyond tonality, noise or improvisation, it remains powerfully indescribable, the sound of ideas having a black mass, or occasionally perhaps, an orgy.

AMM and the Spontaneous Music Ensemble had been convened in a generational moment of experimentation and the work they created and ideas they expressed related to other innovations occurring in the culture.

AMMMusic was released on the Elektra label as part of a deal with Pink Floyd's production company who also credit themselves as AMM's producers on the record. The record label was doubtless uncertain of some of AMM's working methods but their influence on the earliest Pink Floyd recordings is certainly discernible.

Paul McCartney attended an early AMM workshop and, although he found the sessions overlong, he was subsequently inspired to write a fourteen-minute piece of *pop concrète* that became known as Carnival of Light. The composition took its title from 'The Million Volt Light and Shade Rave' where it had been given its solitary performance at a multimedia event at the Roundhouse, a venue that AMM would themselves occasionally play to the bemusement, or more often the apprehension, of the underground *beau monde*.

A few months after the release of *AMMMusic* in 1967, a fissure appeared within the ensemble. Cardew and Rowe were becoming increasingly engaged in Marxist Leninism and their beliefs were consequently informing their musical experiments. Both saw AMM as a potential vehicle for their political philosophy. Disagreements with the other members led to Cardew and Rowe splintering from AMM (Rowe would return in 1975) and the eventual formation of another group, the Scratch Orchestra.

With two other composers, Michael Parsons and Howard Skempton, Cardew had been running workshops at London's Antiuniversity in Shoreditch, as well as at Morley Memorial College for Working Men and Women, an adult education centre near Waterloo that had been established as an act of late-Victorian philanthropy. The Antiuniversity lasted little more than a year and was a high point of the radical energy that had spread across London in the brief flowering of insurrectionary fervour during 1968. Founded in the aftermath of the Dialectics of Liberation conference, the Antiuniversity was located near Old Street in premises that were owned by the Bertrand Russell Peace Foundation and that had formerly been leased to the Vietnam Solidarity Campaign. It was conceived as an open space for learning where anyone, regardless of qualifications or background, could attend lectures and courses for a fee of £8 a quarter. They could do so without the anxiety of being assessed or examined on their subjects and had the right to change their syllabus at any time. The courses were given by some of the era's most notable intellectuals and provocateurs. C. L. R. James ran a course of the history of worker's power, Gustav Metzger taught his theory of auto-destruction with special reference to 'a suicidal faith in the benefits of technology'. R. D. Laing gave lessons in anti-psychiatry and some contemporary accounts state that Aldous Huxley held a seminar on 'How To Stay Alive'. Yoko Ono gave 'an irregular course on connecting people to their own reality by means of brain sessions and ritual'.

Among such distinguished company, Cardew taught workshops to encourage musical self-expression. Out of these sessions he was inspired by the idea of an ensemble or group that could play with little conventional musical aptitude and wrote a draft organisational constitution for a 'Scratch Orchestra':

Definition: A Scratch orchestra is a large number of enthusiasts pooling their resources (not primarily material resources) and assembling for action (music making, performance, edification).

The pianist John Tilbury was a friend, musical collaborator and later a biographer of Cardew, as well as a fellow founding member of the Scratch Orchestra. Tilbury would also later play in AMM. The following description of the Scratch Orchestra, which Tilbury wrote in tribute to Cardew, illustrates the commitment with which its members applied their energy during the Orchestra's brief life.

It was an enterprising body of around forty performers of varied skills, who played all kinds of experimental music – by Cage, Cardew, Wolff, Riley, Young, Rzewski, and themselves –– in all kinds of situations and for all classes of people: for Cornish farm-workers in village squares, for the young industrial workers of the north-east, and for both urban and rural communities on the Continent, as well as for music lovers who frequented the Royal Festival Hall. The Scratch Orchestra consisted of an assortment of people from various walks of life, some of them with considerable artistic talent, who loved and needed music. There was no more enthusiastic, more committed collection of individuals working in the field of contemporary art at that time.

It was to the Scratch Orchestra that Cardew dedicated his next major composition, the large-scale choral work, *The Great Learning*, a setting of one of the key texts of the Confucian religion. *The Great Learning* consists of seven paragraphs that Confucius devoted to the pursuit of moral authority. Cardew gave each of these seven paragraphs an individual setting that allowed for an unlimited number of participants.

Towards the end of 1972 Cardew's politics hardened further. The Scratch Orchestra, having started as an improvisatory collective had evolved into an agitprop group and was disbanded because of disagreements among its members about political strategy. Cardew renounced the avant-garde altogether, a gesture that he made public by publishing the self-critiquing Maoist text *Stockhausen Serves Imperialism*, a virulent attack and repudiation of the majority of the principles and aesthetics that had until then informed his music and his life. In 1973 Cardew became a leading figure in the Communist Party of England (Marxist–Leninist) and engaged in a programme of political activity that would often see him arrested or imprisoned.

Cardew's commitment to revolutionary socialism was as profound as the dedication with which he had applied himself to *Treatise* and *The Great Learning*. During much of the 1970s Cardew could be found playing piano and leading a crowd through anti-fascist songs in community centres in the disaffected areas of inner city London. He would perform at May Day celebrations across Europe and sing republican songs to packed Belfast halls in his school masterly voice. The soft rock group People's Liberation Music was another of Cardew's initiatives. They played accessible versions of 'Peat Bog Soldiers' and Brecht's 'Solidarity Song' from the backs of lorries during marches and demonstrations that faced the National Front head on. As well as arranging and playing the music, Cardew would usually have a hand in the organisation of each meeting and demonstration in which he participated. The fearlessness with which he dedicated himself to what he considered an international struggle was never left unremarked, even by those he had ostracised.

By 1979 the excesses of Maoism had become discredited and Cardew was a founder and member of the central committee of the Revolutionary Communist Party of Britain. Some of his former colleagues, including his previous collaborators in AMM, detected a greater social ease in Cardew along with an overall softening of his character.

Keith Rowe of AMM sensed that although he remained committed against the bourgeois decadence of the avant-garde, Cardew was developing a renewed interest in improvising. Rowe and Eddie Prevost invited the composer to perform *Treatise* once again with a reconfigured AMM. Cardew accepted the invitation and the concert was provisionally booked for the Arnolfini Gallery in Bristol in the spring of 1982, but the performance never took place.

1981 was a year of turbulent domestic politics in the United Kingdom. Inner cities flared with rioting. At Greenham Common a Women's Peace Camp was established in protest against the use of an adjacent RAF base as the site of nuclear warheads and in Belfast's HM Prison Maze, over a period of nine months, ten members of the IRA died on hunger strike. On 13 December Cardew, aged forty-five, was killed in a hit and run. The driver was never caught and the vehicle remained unidentified. Those closest to Cardew, his friends and musical collaborators as well as his comrades in the Revolutionary Communist Party – many of whom were customarily vilified or placed under surveillance as left wing extremists – thought it probable that Cardew, who remained by any definition a highly active political agitator, had been assassinated by MI5.

*

Like Cardew, John Stevens of the Spontaneous Music Ensemble died young, suffering a heart attack in 1994 aged fifty-three. Stevens had concentrated much of his energies in the previous decade on running Community Music, an organisation that he and a partner had founded in order that music could be made accessible to the disenfranchised. Community Music still exists today and enables those with learning difficulties, the elderly and people inhabiting the margins of society to find solace, companionship, possibly even salvation, through the experience of music. Many of the techniques Stevens pioneered during workshops with the Spontaneous Music Ensemble: close listening, deep breathing and the singing of single notes informed the development of Community Music. In 1978 the Open University published *Search and Reflect*, a handbook for music workshops that compiled Stevens's methods into an educational tool.

John Stevens had also often found himself courted by figures from the counter-cultural mainstream. In 1969 he drummed with John Lennon and Yoko Ono at the Natural Music free improvisation concert, a performance that was later released as the album *Unfinished Music No. 2: Life with the Lions* My. In the 1970s Stevens fronted his own jazz-rock band, Away. Later he would perform with John Martyn and Danny Thompson on a tour in the late 1970s that is still legendary for its hedonistic excesses and the aqueous depths of the music.

With *AMMMusic* there was a copy of the second Spontaneous Music Ensemble album *Karyobin* in the back room in Revolver. Although the sleeves lacked the cool lines and orange spines of an Impulse! album or the impeccable design values of Blue Note, they held the beguiling fascination of records that might be a challenging but essentially rewarding experience for the listener.

Karyobin was released in 1968 on Island Records. The front sleeve is printed in a heavy tone of black on which the album title is written in an elegant sans serif.

Underneath is a line of text written in lower case in the same font:

are the imaginary birds said to live in paradise

The lack of a question mark suggested a deeper meaning to the phrase, as if it was part of an overheard conversation or a line from a secret text.

To reinforce the primacy of the music over their personalities, the ensemble inverted music-business orthodoxy and positioned their band name at the least noticeable point of the record cover. Their name appears at the bottom of the sleeve in a typeface so small as to be almost indecipherable.

On the back cover is a photograph of the members of the Spontaneous Music Ensemble that had convened for a day in Olympic Studios London (then the preferred studio of the

Rolling Stones). Although the photograph is in colour, all the members of the Ensemble are dressed in black or black and white. Dave Holland, who would shortly be joining Miles Davis's *Bitches Brew* sessions, holds his double bass. Stevens, seated behind his small drum kit, has the beginning of a beard that he would grow and wear for most of his life. The saxophonist Evan Parker hides behind a thick beard and dark glasses, both of which give him the outward appearance of a contemporary street radical, and to his left the trumpeter Kenny Wheeler stands upright in a jacket and tie. Finally, on the far right of the picture is a seated Derek Bailey who is also wearing a tie and holding his guitar while staring at the camera through his horn-rimmed glasses with the same inscrutable gaze that he would maintain in every photograph taken of him over the next three decades.

The picture lacks the potent imagery found on records made by American contemporaries of the Ensemble. British free players rarely wore dashikis, nor did they make panegyric references to Buddhism in their music; if there is a mysticism inherent in the music of the Spontaneous Music Ensemble, then it is obtuse and unreadable.

At times the Ensemble sounds astringent in its denial of a more chaotic or even cathartic style of playing, but by following Stevens's ideas of listening, the character of the music stands alone. Over their thirty-year existence the Spontaneous Music Ensemble strived for a form of transcendence. Every performance represented a search for some higher truth, one that was attempted by visionaries in Shetland jumpers and steel-rimmed spectacles.

Throughout their working lives Cornelius Cardew and John Stevens remained dedicated to the ideas that they had developed during the 1960s. In Cardew's case this meant a commitment to politics that is often interpreted as having eclipsed his achievements as a composer. As for Stevens, following his instincts and ideas about listening ensured he devoted much of his life encouraging others to do the same.

The dispersal of late 1960s radicalism is often explained as a consequence of the hardening of the state's attitudes after the global political upheaval of 1968. Many of Cardew's and Stevens's contemporaries in other creative spheres withdrew from the confrontational and destabilising experiments of the period and ended the decade in retrenchment. For the Spontaneous Music Ensemble, AMM and their colleagues in free music, the uprisings and *événements* of that year were not so much a culmination of their energies as a point of departure into more extreme aesthetic possibilities and a consolidation of their politics.

Cardew and Stevens were both radicals and their radicalism was such that their work engaged with an audience that existed beyond the arts centres and improv spaces that are the natural home of the British avant-garde. Their ideas and commitment were so rigorous that they managed to reach and affect the more fragile and vulnerable parts of society, where those who had previously thought themselves inarticulate were able to discover a means of self-expression by using methods Stevens and Cardew had assimilated from Ornette Coleman and John Cage.

In the early 1990s the surviving personnel from both AMM and *Karyobin* were regularly producing CDs and collaborations.

Along with workshops and Arts Council commissions, musicians such as Evan Parker, Derek Bailey and Trevor Watts and the rest of Stevens and Cardew's contemporaries all shared an ability to self-organise and maintain a form of anti-career. They often founded record labels to release their and their associates' music. These record companies were usually run from the spare bedroom in houses they had bought cheaply in pre-gentrification north-east London and were given names like 'Incus', 'Pogus' and 'Tangent'.

The music they recorded was in the exploratory tradition of 1960s improv and retained the uncompromising will of the era although many of them were now drawing breath for their instruments with the helpful addition of a paunch. Once a month or so Kenneth Ansell from Impetus would collect sample copies of their latest releases into a briefcase, settle into his Morris Minor Clubman and drive an hour across the Isle of Lewis from Skigersta to Stornoway. There he would take the ferry from the Hebrides across the North Sea to the Scottish mainland and slowly begin the drive that would end at the door of Revolver, where he would attempt to sell us the latest offerings from what was left of the British improv underground in their middle years.

*

Upon entering the doorway into the shop, Ken had the unmistakable air of a person halfway through a six-hundred-mile round trip across Britain; the sole purpose of which was an attempt to garner interest in a handful of new releases from what was conventionally regarded as the rather marginal genre of improvised British free jazz. Dressed in his usual combination of sheepskin jacket and corduroys, Ken headed towards the counter with a confidence that could not quite disguise a trace of resignation. Along with his familiar attire Ken was easily identified by his beard and thousand-yard stare – the kind that only the probing self-examination that inevitably accompanies a long drive can legitimately produce.

The first words that greeted Ken as he made himself known to anyone behind the counter tended to be 'No' followed by 'No' in quick succession. Roger had firmly indicated to the rest of the staff that we were on no account in a financial position to show any interest in any of Ken's wares. It was usually Roger who dealt with Ken. On seeing him approach the counter Roger might make a friendly shooing gesture to accompany the vehement shaking of his head.

'We haven't got any money,' Roger would say, smiling. 'Sorry.'

Undeterred, and with the hard-won authority of an old frontiersman who had reached the point of no return, Ken would start inspecting the contents of his leather suitcase that he had placed, somewhat assertively, on the shop counter.

Avoiding any eye contact, Ken quickly produced three copies of *The Wire* from the depths of his case; these he placed airily on the counter before us. This opening gambit succeeded both as a delaying tactic and as a method of testing whether, beneath the air of friendly hostility, Roger might be prepared to accommodate some of Ken's latest releases. Distracted, at times perplexed and at times, it has to be said, greatly amused by whichever cover star *The Wire* had chosen for that month's issue, Roger and I would be scanning through the magazine with a long-rehearsed combination of curiosity and scepticism.

While we were preoccupied by *The Wire* for a moment, Ken, now outside our peripheral vision, started writing in his note pad.

In a fine hand he noted down the day's date and in the left column he wrote 'Revolver'. In the right-hand column, now with the flourish of a fisherman casting out towards signs of activity beneath the current, he added 'The Wire X 3 F.O.C.'

By now Roger had headed in to the back room and tossed his copy of *The Wire* into his shoulder bag, muttering about the need to reorganise his plans for the evening. Aware that he had bought himself some time, Ken quickly delved back into his case and built a diminutive stack of sample CDs on the counter over which his right hand hovered as if ready for the draw. As he returned to the counter, Roger made his feelings about Ken's decision to insist on showing us his wares clearly known.

'I just told you,' said Roger. 'We haven't got any money.'

Although his head was nodding with the sympathy one might expect from a counsellor, Ken's face now wore a half-smile, giving the impression that the advantage was now with him.

'I'd like to know what you think of this,' he said, as he handed Roger a CD by an ominous pan-European sounding trio of free-jazz journeymen.

'Perhaps not as complex in its arrangements as some of us may have been expecting.'

Roger, while indicating with a fixed moue that Ken's attempt at a charm offensive was rather ill-judged, almost desperate, could not resist this invitation to pass judgement on a forthcoming release and inserted Ken's offering into the CD player.

A silence descended upon the shop. It was past six and the sense of another day's trading drawing to an end was palpable as Roger made some of his familiar micro-adjustments to the volume on the stereo.

After a few minutes some closely recorded cymbals

skittered into life. With little warning a tenor saxophone aggressively asserted itself. The saxophone player and the drummer began to improvise with the sort of discordant tones suggestive of protracted marital breakdown; a guitarist, presumably located in a building adjacent to his fellow musicians, began gamely attacking his instrument with, it was fair to assume, a hammer.

Roger, having spent a short while closely absorbed in the trio's efforts, was now ready with a précis: 'Well . . .'

An unexpected but wholly unnecessary change in musical direction, one that involved the drummer deciding to walk across his cymbals and drum kit, prompted a pause in Roger's response.

'I mean . . . playing it a bit safe, aren't they?' he continued, as the sound of the night shift at an abattoir going about its business emerged from the shop's speakers. 'Bit polite, isn't it?' 'I think so,' replied Ken. 'I really do think so.'

As Roger returned the CD with a dismissive shake of the head, Ken was ready with what he felt might be a more engaging suggestion from the current Impetus list.

'Try this instead,' he said. 'It's a set of solo table-top guitar pieces from someone who's worked closely with Keiji Haino. It's not really a noise recording – it's more nuanced than that, there are vocal elements as well. It was put together in a disused temple.'

Roger, now hitting his stride as an expert in free music's direction of travel, pressed play once more and shifted his weight in preparation for what Ken's relaxed posture at the counter suggested might be a new chapter in table-top guitar improv.

A few seconds later the shop stereo emitted a bloodcurdling scream. This, it soon became apparent, was a prelude to the sound of a long-forgotten 78 record, one that on first listen may have been a recording of an opera, being pushed back and forth under a phonograph needle with a highly convincing degree of commitment.

The screams continued in counterpoint to the now emerging aria, the reimagined setting of which now evoked the foreboding climax of a badly organised witch trial.

'Yes,' Roger said, his head nodding. 'Better, much better.'

'The table-top comes in a moment or two, if I remember correctly,' said Ken, at which point some indeterminate but baleful machinery began a twenty-minute extemporisation on what the table-top guitar player doubtless thought was a highly personal investigation into psychic pain.

'Go on then,' said Roger. 'You can put us down for one of these.'

And so the process by which Ken managed never to leave Revolver empty-handed began.

Ken would guide us through his assorted micro-genres: live recordings of Sun Ra, duo recordings of guitar and drums, orchestral works by fading avant-garde composers and almost always, the latest offering from a former contemporary, band mate or collaborator of Cornelius Cardew or John Stevens.

A week or so later a jiffy bag with an Outer Hebridean postmark would be in the morning's post. Half a dozen or so CDs would be enclosed with a hand-written invoice. I would price up the delivery, file the CDs in master bags behind the counter and place the cases in the new releases section of the shop's ever-lengthening improv and free-jazz section. And there they would remain. In all my time spent behind the counter I can remember no more than a scant four or five customers finding it necessary to browse, let alone purchase any of the stock we ordered from Ken. Roger would occasionally come across an invoice from Impetus amid the gathering piles of delivery notes and other paper detritus. He would briefly stare at Ken's handwriting and start shaking his head at the amount.

'We can't keep doing this,' he said, as he pointed towards the far wall of the shop that was now permanently overstocked with definitive avant-garde recordings by middle-aged men. 'It just sits there.'

Bristol on a bright spring morning often felt rich with promise. I would walk the half mile or so to Revolver from my cold-water flat absentmindedly, lost in wonder at the thought of another day spent there and the endless possibility of the hours immersed in whatever music we might choose to listen to. As I opened the door and switched off the alarm, I gathered up the post at my feet. Bound together by a rubber band was the usual batch of invoices, late-payment reminders and circulars that tended to be neglected as soon as they were stuffed in a drawer behind the counter. Among them was a folded A2 poster for the forthcoming Bath International Music Festival.

I scoured the names listed on the programme and saw that Eddie Prevost of AMM, the saxophonist Evan Parker whose name I recognised from the back of the sleeve of the Spontaneous Music Ensemble's *Karyobin* and the American pianist Marilyn Crispell were performing at the festival as a trio. I added the poster to the layer of fading flyers and out-of-date adverts for previous concerts that surrounded the shop's doorway and heard the familiar clacking of Roger's bike being lifted up the stairs. He wandered over to see what had inspired me to go to such great lengths as putting up a poster, the type of altruistic activity that tended to be frowned upon.

'Prevost . . . Parker . . . Crispell,' Roger read out the names slowly. 'We should go.'

I stood near the entrance to Revolver gazing at the May evening scene; the shops on Park Street had shut for the day and in the handful of cafés and restaurants up and down the hill trade was slow. At moments such as this, when the sunlight lingered on its quiet, broad streets and cast its buildings in a dusty amber, it was difficult not to accept that part of Bristol's charm lay in its lassitude.

A briskly driven small car parked very near my feet. 'Quick,' shouted Roger. 'They're on in half an hour!' In a matter of ten or so minutes we were driving along the

A4 to Bath and I was struck by the fact that for once our transport was not Roger's white van but a car, presumably borrowed. 'I'd better check where the lights are on this,' he said, largely to himself, as he put the various switches and controls through their paces, 'for when we drive back tonight.'

The windscreen wipers came on, at first slowly, then at a great pace. The car in front was accidentally beeped by the horn and then, in what the driver of the car in front no doubt regarded as an act of great provocation, was flashed repeatedly by Roger who had finally located the headlight switches.

'Sorry!' Roger shouted, while waving his hand in apology, his face settled in a benign grin. The car in front showed no response. With little other traffic in sight, Roger produced a recently opened bottle of wine from the storage compartment in the door. After having taken a furtive swig he passed the bottle over to me. 'It was sitting on the kitchen table,' he said by way of an explanation. 'Right, we need to find somewhere to park.'

*

In the first half of *Northanger Abbey*, Jane Austen uses the Upper Assembly Rooms in Bath as the location for the journey her heroine Catherine Morland takes through the vibrant snobbery of society and its attendant balls.

In chapter two Catherine and her host Mrs Allen make their first visit of the summer season. Unfortunately, upon arrival at the Upper Rooms, they find themselves among unfamiliar company and are left to rely on the good grace and charity of their neighbours at the tea-room table.

'How uncomfortable it is,' whispered Catherine, 'not to have a single acquaintance here!'

'Yes, my dear,' replied Mrs Allen, with perfect serenity, 'it is very uncomfortable indeed.'

'What shall we do? – The gentlemen and ladies at this table look as if they wondered why we came here – we seem forcing ourselves into their party.'

'Aye, so we do – That is very disagreeable. I wish we had a large acquaintance here.'

'I wish we had any; – it would be somebody to go to.'

By chapter ten, however, Catherine and Mrs Allen have formed new friendships among the tea rooms and balls, including one with the Tilneys and their eldest son Henry, and a few weeks into the season, Austen's heroine is now quite at ease in the gaiety of the Upper Rooms.

Miss Tilney met her (Catherine) with great civility, returned her advances with equal good will, and they continued talking together as long as both parties remained in the room: and though in all probability not an observation was made, nor an expression used by either which had not been made and used some thousands of time before, under that roof, in every Bath season, yet the merit of their being spoken with simplicity and truth, and without personal conceit, might be something uncommon.

'How well your brother dances!' was an artless exclamation of Catherine's towards the close of their conversation, which at once surprized and amused her companion.

'Henry!' she replied with a smile. 'Yes, he does dance very well.'

As Roger and I approached the Assembly Rooms that May evening, little of the building's appearance had outwardly changed since the early summer evenings that Austen had described in her first novel with its nods to the Gothic.
The twilight shone through the high windows and a low murmur was audible from the rooms as we made our way through the entrance.

Here, the contrast in the purpose of our visit and those of Catherine Morland, Mrs Allen, the Tilneys and their friends became more pronounced. Rather than the lively dances and card tables populated with debutantes and chaperones who, Austen suggests, might be at their happiest when discussing muslin, on the evening of our visit the ballroom was occupied by a mainly male audience, almost all of whom were dressed in the informal 'Ken from Impetus' style.

Roger approached the bar with his usual self-confidence and asked for two glasses, and into these, with just a hint of surreptitiousness, he poured the remainder of the bottle of wine we had begun to share in the car.

A Revolver regular, a tender man and one of several of those around us sporting a healthy if not necessarily well-groomed beard, approached us with visible enthusiasm. 'This should be special,' he said. 'This could really go somewhere. And we could go there with them.'

I looked around the hall and saw further reminders that I had never before attended the sort of a performance our friend was anticipating. There were gilt-backed plastic seats with red cushions that had been carefully laid out by the commissars of the Assembly Rooms, and the floor had been recently polished. Although it held a grand piano, along with a complex drum kit and percussion stand, the dais on the stage was reminiscent of an end-of-term prize giving.

Milling around the bar or leaning with their backs against the newly painted walls, the audience of around two hundred, if not especially well-heeled, were certainly respectable and evidently anticipating some form of musical insurrection. Such was the conviction of their body language and the growing excitement in the tone of their conversation that it was hard not to assume that the evening would conclude in some form of societal upheaval.

Roger smiled at the odd familiar face from Revolver and began nodding his head in approval at the atmosphere that was developing. As he took in the room, he turned to me and said, 'We just need Evan to have brought his tenor.'

I was not altogether sure what he had meant by this, but I nodded slowly while staring idly at the parquet floor. This seemed both a polite response and also fairly indicative of typical jazz behaviour. Nearby a tannoy crackled into life and a few seconds later a mellifluous voice urged us to take our seats, and did so at an unusually civilised volume.

For most of the first half the trio played around rather than across one another. Marilyn Crispell would improvise some clusters on the piano and Eddie Prevost, who stood rather than sat at his drum kit and percussion, accompanied them respectfully. Evan Parker's saxophone punctuated any gaps his colleagues had left and gradually the energy between the musicians increased. During the last fifteen minutes before the interval Parker concentrated on playing only a handful of notes and Crispell treated her piano more as a percussive instrument. Her hands attacked the keyboard with growing malevolence. Clearly inspired by the increasing physicality of her approach, Prevost set upon his cymbals with timpani mallets, the effect of which was to fill the Assembly Rooms with the sound.

As the trio left the stage, a stillness lingered around the empty dais. An undertone of whispered reaction gradually gave way to vigorous applause. This lasted until some preordained moment in the audience's subconscious when, as one, the crowd made their way to the bar. Their eyes were radiant with pleasure and expectation and as they formed an orderly queue their heads made amiable but insistent nods toward one another.

Crispell began the second half with a solo piano improvisation. Her hair was bobbed and her dress was floral-patterned, but the way in which she laid waste to the grand piano suggested a temperament that was far from the pastoral. Her whole arm would slam down repeatedly across the keyboard while her other hand systematically punched at the same cluster of notes with unreasonable insistence. By the end of her set the energy in the Assembly Rooms had undergone a palpable transformation; having absorbed the audience's ovation with a modest smile and a seated bow, Crispell, with her head in her hands, watched from her piano as Parker stepped towards the front of the stage.

'Yes,' Roger said to me in a half whisper. 'Evan's brought his tenor.'

The lights in the Assembly Rooms were now brighter than the daylight that was fading in its windows.

Other than the constant motion of his head and the interplay of his hands, Parker stood motionless holding his tenor saxophone underneath the Georgian candelabra whose lustre was reflected in its body. He began by gradually teasing the odd terse squall from his instrument. These strained notes were short in length and he also started using his hands in a percussive manner similar to the one Crispell had used on her piano. His right hands flicked and tapped at the saxophone keys as his left hand was a blur of movement. These actions seemed to have little in common with the length or tone of the sound he was producing. In parallel with Parker's high-register filigrees, an uneven drone had started to drift across the Assembly Rooms. At first I assumed a member of the audience had become so overawed by the evening that they had fallen into an invocatory trance. The drone grew stronger and was certainly now coming form the stage. I gave Roger a perplexed look.

'Circular breathing,' he whispered.

Although its name suggests an activity that might be related to speaking in tongues, circular breathing is a method by which air can be temporarily stored – for seconds – in the cheeks of a horn player. In essence circular breathing is simultaneously inhaling and exhaling, circumventing the lungs by using the face muscles to expel air separately, and it was this surplus exhalation that was producing the non-material sound of the drone.

As it floated in the air above our heads, the doleful tone felt like a summons to prayer. Although intermittent, it seemed to penetrate every available space in the room and create the benign autosuggestion in each member of the audience that allowed us to breathe as one.

Suddenly a brutal percussive noise cut through the

meditative undercurrent and Prevost began accompanying Parker once more. Standing over his percussion in a leather jacket and with cropped hair, he had the air of a veteran *enragé*; the dexterity with which he produced harsh clangs and explosive snaps out of his drums indicated an unhesitating sense of purpose. Within minutes Crispell had once more started attacking her piano. Compared to the first set they now inhabited a markedly changed temporal reality. Suddenly Prevost produced a violin bow that he dragged gently across his cymbals with one arm, as his other hand skittered across the tom toms as if he were attempting to keep them at bay. The piano was producing thunderclaps and Parker was emitting a sound on his saxophone that, to all of us present in the Assembly Rooms, represented a finely wrought musical freedom.

As the trio acknowledged the audience's applause refracted light from the chandeliers danced across the Assembly Room's polished floor.

On the drive home Roger and I sat silently in the car with our thoughts submerged.

After ten or so minutes of quiet contemplation Roger began speaking with a noticeable grain of sentiment in his voice.

'I've never seen anyone produce white noise from a drum kit like that before,' he said.

'They all seemed to be listening to each other through that noise,' I suggested.

'You have to listen with improv,' Roger continued. 'It's what isn't there that makes it interesting. They can't produce anything like we saw tonight without thinking about all the spaces in between. They have to leave things and do without.'

He started smiling, and his eyes wandered away from the windscreen and across to the outskirts of Bristol where the city started to flatten and condense.

'Like we all do.'

7

The stereo in Revolver was set behind the counter in a recess that had once held a fireplace and was enclosed by the whitewashed floor-to-ceiling chimneybreast. The cavity offered room enough for a turntable, CD player and cassette deck along with two or three shelves of vinyl. On the wall above the stereo hung a large PVC display sheet that was divided into forty sections, each of which contained a 7" single.

The shop's point of sale was the counter, the antithesis of what the retail industry might consider a dynamic and professional trading environment. Nevertheless, in a nod to the conventions of music retailing, we endeavoured to keep this display above the stereo continually stocked with interesting records. Rare singles were inserted near the top of the wall, which in an accidental act of purchasing psychology meant that anyone glancing at them had to look up and slightly strain their neck to appreciate their value, scarcity and historical significance.

For the customer, staring at this wall of vinyl and gazing at the myriad colours and designs of the rows of 7" singles had a similar effect to that of looking at the jars on the shelves of a well-stocked confectioner's. The wall display also had another function. It gave anyone standing at the counter a justification to appear preoccupied by its contents and provided them with an excuse not to engage with, or perhaps more truthfully, not to endure, our commentary about their purchases.

Occasionally singles from the wall seemed unable to generate any interest, even to a clientele as unpredictable as ours. Perhaps because of its monochromatic sleeve, one 7" in particular struggled to capture anyone's imagination. 'Pristine Christine' by the Sea Urchins was certainly a lovingly assembled record. Its cover had been neatly folded over and inserted into a PVC sleeve. This contained a 7" single with a bright red-and-yellow label on to which were printed a drawing of some flowers and, in capital letters reminiscent of a child's building blocks, 'S A R A H 1'. As well as providing a visual counterpoint to the black-and-white record sleeve, these primary colours felt peculiarly assertive, although their impact was offset by the inclusion of a monochrome poster that had been enclosed with the record. The poster was printed on fairly high-quality paper and showed the Sea Urchins in a variety of poses and situations that, as is often the way with a band's debut release, placed great emphasis on their hairstyles.

One solitary afternoon I realised that I had sat or stood in close proximity to this record for around five months and felt suddenly obliged, considering all the hours I had passed in its company, to listen to it.

Up until this particular moment of languor, a feeling of deflation and hopelessness had accompanied the thought of playing 'Pristine Christine'. Despite the attention to detail that had gone into its manufacture, the imagery on the sleeve felt overfamiliar. On the cover the band were photographed looking rather wan and they wore the mandatory signifiers of young provincial guitar groups on small independent labels: polo necks, fringes, leather jackets and a contrived air of insouciance.

In Revolver we liked to think that, if nothing else, we were a jazz shop, a reggae shop and a shop that stocked music from the farthest limits of music's imagination. Notwithstanding our joy at often sharing such conceits with the occasional customer, we were also frequently an empty shop; but with the music of the spheres, or at least our interpretation of it, permanently available at one's fingertips. Summoning the energy to play a 7" by a long (but perhaps justifiably) overlooked guitar band such as the Sea Urchins felt like an unnecessary intrusion into an hour spent idly sitting on a stool and staring into space.

With an inward sigh I managed to overcome such instinctive disinclination and summoned the will to place the needle on 'Pristine Christine'. The song was six years old and had been released in 1987, a year after C86, the rather random grouping of tentative, or in some cases disobliging, guitar bands from which the Sea Urchins had obviously taken much of their influence. It sounded not so much dated as arcane. The singer's voice was lachrymose but suggested that he lacked the necessary energy or perhaps even the will to summon any tears. An unkind verdict, the type that an indolent record shop assistant could make with the gravitas and authority of a QC, might be that the self-consciousness that had gone into the creation of 'Pristine Christine' was so overwrought that any distinction between naïve and faux-naif had become lost.

As I found myself playing the single once more and then again for a third time, my prejudices gradually began to wilt. Beneath the song's stylised bashfulness was a compelling and melodic urgency; the guitars were played with a sense of purpose and whatever the band's debt to the affectations of C86, the Sea Urchins, at least on the basis of three consecutive listens to their debut single, certainly had an engaging charm.

I replaced 'Pristine Christine' on the wall and noticed that at my feet was another record that had also been more or less stationary for the best part of a year: a worn but presentable copy of 'If Only I Could Remember My Name', the debut solo album by David Crosby.

While a founder of The Byrds, Crosby had helped pioneer both the chiming guitar timbre beloved of bands such as the Sea Urchins as well as the ubiquitous fringed haircut sported by many of the pale young men who played in that style.

Upon the release of 'If Only I Could Remember My

Name' Crosby had long been dismissed from the Byrds and was now a member of Crosby, Stills & Nash (occasionally with Young), a supergroup, their contemporaries noted, whose name also suggested an ambitious new legal practice. Their music provided congenial insulation against the fading dreams of the Age of Aquarius and the encroaching reality of rising commodity prices in a society that was now less well off. Crosby, Stills, Nash & Young's success was spectacular; as the 1960s ended they provided a bridge into the new decade by writing songs about bourgeois hippie domesticity: fixing up houses, holidaying in Morocco and teaching children to love one another.

'If Only I Could Remember My Name' was a markedly less sentimental record than those Crosby made as a member of his supergroup. It was the work of a damaged psyche, one that was attempting to find a degree of solace in meditative, sometimes only partly formed, songs. The ruthless and competitive professionalism of Crosby, Stills, Nash & Young was entirely absent from Crosby's solo album. Instead it sounded as if some half-remembered thoughts had been recorded late into the night in the hope that come the morning their meaning might be revealed.

Some of the initial sessions for 'If Only I Could Remember My Name' had begun in Los Angeles, but most of the album was deliberately recorded at a distance from the West Coast recording industry in San Francisco, where Crosby lived on a houseboat moored nearby in Sausalito. The cover of the album is a close-up of Crosby superimposed on a burnished sea sunset: we see the singer staring out across the waves and we are invited to share his view.

At its most simplistic 'If Only I Could Remember My Name' is the sound of Crosby jamming until morning with fellow members of the late 1960s' Californian musical nobility. Many of the songs start with the just discernible sound of the studio tape being punched in, an indication that a record is being made in the moment. Loosely picked guitars slowly settle on a rhythm as Joni Mitchell, Neil Young, members of the Grateful Dead, Quicksilver Messenger Service, Crosby's band mates and Jefferson Airplane all make significant contributions, many of which only reveal themselves upon repeated and careful listening. A picture was circulated to promote the release, a colour-saturated photograph of everyone involved in the record's creation sitting in stoned, communal contemplation in the small control room at Wally Heider's studio. Rather than highlight the august cast Crosby had assembled, the picture has the feeling of intrusion. The faces and identities are hard to determine and the more one studies the image the more difficult it is to establish who is in the room. All those present share a dress sense and a particular air of detachment, one, the photograph suggests, that has been initiated by a rarefied and uninhibited set of experiences.

Whenever he travelled between the two cities, Crosby

would break the journey between Los Angeles and San Francisco at Big Sur. He made these road trips in a Volkswagen camper van that had been fitted with a Porsche engine. It is hard to imagine a more apposite metaphor for the contradictory impulses that were disorientating his generation. At Big Sur he would combine restorative contemplation in the Pacific Redwood wilderness with enquiries about the availability of any real estate. The area had long held a fascination, both for its calm and iridescent beauty and as a locus for what had become known as the human potential movement, a series of practices and beliefs that placed an emphasis on consciousness-raising techniques.

These ideas had been developed on the Big Sur coastline at Esalen Institute, a former motel and hot springs resort, that in 1962 was converted into a research centre to examine and develop the theory of human potential.

The activities at Esalen attracted a regular stream of visitors and lecturers including Aldous Huxley, Joan Baez and Buckminster Fuller, figures whose public profiles ensured that the experiments in lifestyle conducted at the Institute entered the mainstream as fundamental tenets of the counter-culture and, a decade after it had opened, that Esalen had a reputation as its holding point.

In July 1969, two weeks after Woodstock where Crosby, Stills & Nash had played their second-ever concert to almost half a million people, the band set up their equipment around the swimming pool at Esalen Institute and performed in front of an audience of little over a thousand.

The concert was filmed as *Celebration at Big Sur* and included footage of Crosby and some friends naked in the institute's natural hot springs and watching the waves break on the rocks beneath Esalen. In one scene Crosby is leading his fellow bathers through a communal chant of 'om'. Hours spent listening to 'If Only I Could Remember My Name' suggest that in the recording studio an equally submerged Crosby was attempting to locate his own personal root note of transcendence.

Two songs on 'If Only I Could Remember My Name' are wordless and consist of Crosby chanting or scat singing to his open-tuned guitar. In the right circumstances, listening to these pieces is soothing and restive, an almost spiritual activity. One of these, 'I'd Swear There Was Somebody Here' is the sound of Crosby's voice alone, multitracked into a slowly vanishing haze. It is little over a minute and a half long and ends in a series of high notes. The audible strain in Crosby as he reaches for these final phrases is both the burden they place on his register and the emotional pain he is attempting to expel; stoned listeners might convince themselves they were listening to the sound of a falling star, a more sober reaction might be that on 'If Only I Could Remember My Name' Crosby created a form of Californian plainsong.

At almost eight minutes 'Cowboy Movie' is the album's

longest song. A stream of consciousness description of a gang of outlaws on a mythical Western plain, its narrative does not bear close scrutiny but the intensity of Crosby's delivery is remarkable. Throughout the song his voice levels vary, so that in some passages he is obviously swaying in front of the microphone. The structure of 'Cowboy Movie' is as vacillating as its lyrics but the song has a momentum propelled by Crosby's performance.

In the same year that Crosby produced his solo record his friend Dennis Hopper released his own interpretation of a cowboy film, *The Last Movie*, the long-delayed follow-up to the highly successful *Easy Rider*. In contrast to its predecessor that had won the Palme d'Or at Cannes, *The Last Movie* was denigrated. Rather than being viewed as influenced by experimental European cinema, Hopper's use of jump cuts and disconnected sequences was dismissed as drug-fuelled incoherence and *The Last Movie* was criticised for such perceived flaws. The film's million-dollar budget became symbolic of the director's boundless excess and it was reported that the coterie around Hopper had treated the film's Peru location as an opportunity for an extended vacation amidst the director's mental and narcotic collapse.

It was an article of faith between its auteurs and their circle of producers and acolytes that in *Easy Rider* Hopper had based his character's wardrobe and moustache on Crosby. The intervening two years had had such an effect on their imagination that they were both now simultaneously adrift in hallucinatory cowboy landscapes largely impenetrable to anyone outside their confidence.

Decades later the Internet and cultural heritage industries would allow the significance of both *The Last Movie* and 'If Only I Could Remember My Name' to be revised, and the film and the album would each receive a mild form of beatification.

As I regarded the original copy of the album lying at my feet I was struck by how little interest it generated in our customers. I thought one of us might eventually be adequately motivated to place it in the second-hand racks, where it would be ignored on that side of the counter as much as it had been here.

The David Crosby record had become as overfamiliar and unwanted an item as the copy of 'Pristine Christine' I now decided to play for a fourth time. Although made only four or five years later than The Byrds records that influenced them, 'If Only I Could Remember My Name' had remained unacknowledged by the Sea Urchins and their contemporaries who had dismissed such lesser known works as hippyish overspill. Its opaque, contemplative depths were lost to the generation that had been stylised by *C86* and who now conflated concise, treble-heavy love songs with the morality and parsimony of punk rock.

'Pristine Christine' was the first single released on a Bristol record label, Sarah Records, a company that was hard to disassociate from the faded gentility of the city. The label had two founders, Clare Wadd and Matt Haynes, who had both come to Bristol as undergraduates. Matt would occasionally venture into the shop with a box of Sarah stock that he offered to us for sale or return. He was rather tall and a little shy and wore his hair in a parted fringe long enough to half cover his features. Like so many before him, his body language as he approached the counter suggested that he had carefully considered whether a visit to Revolver was strictly necessary.

Any insults he suffered in his dealings with us were balanced by a rather qualified but genuine affection we held for the label. Their releases were routinely vilified in the music papers where their house style of music, a wilfully fey and capricious form of guitar pop, was often criticised in language that veered towards homophobia and sexism. The most beguiling aspect of the label was that, like us, Wadd and Haynes had built a parallel universe for themselves in a corner of this quiet city. The private world of Revolver consisted of selling, buying and arguing about records. For Sarah theirs consisted of releasing music, mainly on 7" singles, and dispatching them with accompanying letters to their customers in the manner of a pen-pal correspondence.

Sarah perfected insularity. Through a combination of ignorance and ambivalence the label was almost entirely disengaged from the music industry and Wadd and Haynes shared these inhibitions with the bands they released and the fans of the label with whom they corresponded. As

Sarah was based in Bristol rather than London, the media was aware that it was unlikely to come into contact with either of Sarah's proprietors socially, and regularly treated the label as an object of its prejudices and hostility. Wadd and Haynes's attitude hardened accordingly, with the result that their provincialism flourished into an art form.

Sarah released compilations of their 7" singles with titles taken from locations around Bristol and with sleeves that featured photographs of some of its more intriguing cityscapes. The first compilation was released in 1988 and named *Shadow Factory* after a Second World War aircraft wing-manufacturer's in the suburb of Filton. Its catalogue number was 587, after the number of the bus route that led there, and its sleeve was a picture of one of Bristol's harbour developments. Part of the overall Sarah project was a remapping of the city in this style, one that altered its boundaries in line with the label founders' imagination.

The final Sarah release was a retrospective compilation titled *There and Back Again Lane* after a Clifton side street located just around the corner from Revolver. One of Sarah's most prominent bands, the Field Mice, had once paid a visit to the shop. They had doubtless anticipated a friendly reception and may have expected warm conversation about the nuances of life as members of the wider independent music community. Unfortunately the environment in Revolver was rather more hostile to such badinage than the Field Mice had perhaps imagined. In this instance it verged on the antagonistic, so much so that a member of the band was almost reduced to tears.

Occasionally the shop was more supportive. As she made her rounds around the Bristol stores Clare Wadd once visited Revolver with a new release, *Le Jardin de Heavenly*, along with an armful of accompanying promotional material. Instead of assuring her that a poster or two might be accommodated on the wall, she was encouraged by a member of staff to decorate the entire shop in Heavenly artwork. For the remainder of Revolver's life it was always possible to see small strips from the cover artwork of *Le Jardin de Heavenly* on patches of the shop walls.

As well as being its principal visual and linguistic signifier, the city felt in tune with the manner in which Sarah functioned as a record label. Although only three of the bands they worked with were based in Bristol, each record the company released felt imbued with a particular gentleness, one that might be attributed to certain parts of the city, particularly its sleepy back streets, from where Sarah assembled and distributed its catalogue.

There was also a timorous quality in the music Sarah released. Some of the label's most characteristic songs such as 'Emma's House' by the Field Mice shared the same sense of subdued melancholy as an evening walk through Bristol. In the same way in which hearing first generation hip-hop played through boomboxes was an example of musical *genius loci* in the Bronx, listening to 'Emma's House' with its lyrics about 'Early morning by the harbour' on cheap headphones, while strolling along the quays at the Arnolfini, had its own authenticity of experience.

As was so often the case with small independent record companies in the 1980s, Sarah gave great prominence to sleeve design and the visual identity of the label. Wadd and Haynes collaborated with their bands to produce record covers rich in primary or pastel colours and Letraset-style fonts. These designs would be assembled and made camera-ready by Wadd and Haynes at home; they would then carry the artwork through the Bristol drizzle to the printers in Clifton Village that produced their sleeves. At the print shop the plastic bags that had covered their large improvised cardboard portfolio would be stripped away and Wadd and Haynes would start their discussions about Pantones and paper stock with the printers.

Clifton Print was more accustomed to producing lightly embossed wedding invitations or dinner menus for functions, so the requests Sarah made for overlaid colours and tinted photo reproductions ensured that the label stood out from their usual stock. Together with their fold-over record sleeves Clifton Print also produced the newsletters that the label regularly produced in editions of a thousand and regularly mailed to their correspondents.

Although the newsletters were printed in the Sarah designs of bright colours and their back page featured a set of paw tracks, their editorial content was often noticeable for its trenchant opinions, which on occasion could turn vehement. There was an ideology within the label. In certain aspects it was an intensified version of the usual independent record company concerns: refusing to work with major labels, allowing the bands creative freedom and insisting that the market come to Sarah rather than the reverse. In Wadd and Haynes's case this stance was admirably unwavering throughout the label's history. They also rightly drew on the significance of being an equal partnership in a sector still rife with sexism and one in which very few women were in positions of authority.

These principles were coupled with Sarah's isolation from the conventional music industry to such an extent that the label could occasionally give the impression of leading a sect or a faith community. Their newsletters often included the customary indie accusations of 'sell-out' and 'middle-class lifestyle', gestures that were occasionally met with wry smiles, as it was rumoured in Bristol that the house Sarah operated from had been purchased by one of their parents.

Although their commitment to independence was often dismissed as dilettantish or infantile, Sarah was widely respected for the integrity it so cherished. It may well have been the only record company to have the honour of John Peel playing every 7" single that it released.

*

My flat in Bristol was a one-room studio on the first floor of a large Victorian terrace in a slightly shabby street in Clifton. The landlord occupied the top of the house that included an enormous, high attic that was accessed by a small rickety staircase. Along with indeterminate sentimental chaff the attic was filled with furniture, books, magazines and large oil canvases that he was storing for a friend. The attic was illuminated by original but filthy glass ceiling windows that allowed in enough daylight to catch the dust motes hanging in the air. There was no fixed policy in terms of whom the landlord accepted as tenants; his sole criterion was that he recognised in them a shared sense of humour. My landlord's great love was the Marx Brothers, and he would occasionally pay tribute to their impulsive humour by changing hats throughout the day. One afternoon he arrived to do some rewiring in a Cossack bearskin hat. Half an hour later he returned upstairs in search of a different set of screws and re-emerged sporting a trilby. Once the wall socket had been replaced he promised to return that evening to run a circuit check, which he duly did while wearing a beret.

Perhaps in homage to Marx Brothers slapstick or to the films of Billy Wilder which he would also watch and re-watch regularly, the landlord had installed a pull-down bed located in a wall closet in each flat. If I arrived home late at night I rarely trusted myself with the bed's sprung mechanism. Instead I would often hastily improvise a bed made of chair cushions and whatever else was to hand.

One morning I was lying on the floor in one such improvised berth when the ringing of the phone interrupted my sleep. I shifted my head to listen as the answering machine clicked into life. The voice was familiar although it was one that I had not previously heard on a telephone:

'Hello, this is John Peel, I was ringing about . . .'

Before the caller could finish his sentence I picked up the receiver and hurriedly began making my apologies for screening my phone calls and explained that I was suffering from the after effects of a late night.

'Oh, good, anywhere fun?' he asked.

I paused for the shortest of moments before answering, as I realised that my reply was likely to have an effect.

'Well,' I said 'I went to see the Fall, actually.'

A silence descended, during which I became aware of the physical distance between our two telephones. I began to wonder if he thought I was being flippant or sarcastic.

'Tell me,' he said in a quieter and more measured voice than the one he had previously been using, 'were they any good?'

I ran through my memories of the previous evening. My hangover was now tempered by the realisation that I was suddenly being confided in. I mentioned that the only words Mark E. Smith had said all night were 'In the age of Richard and Judy, we are the Fall' and that the band, who were undergoing one of their more settled periods, sounded lean and purposeful, and that their use of sequencers and keyboards in particular had made them seem powerful but also a little removed.

Peel took this in with a series of murmured sighs and affirmative grunts, sounds that one might associate with a parent casting their eye over a child's end of year report. I had also mentioned that it was one of the few occasions I had seen whole families – mothers, fathers and sons – together at a concert.

'Oh, we do that,' said Peel. 'Last week we hired a minibus to go together and see the Fall play in Ipswich.' His voice started to fade. 'And I have to say that they weren't all that good.'

'Well, thanks for that,' he continued. 'The reason I'm calling is that I have enjoyed reading the insert to the latest Planet Records release, especially news about Teenagers In Trouble and their forthcoming cover version of the entire *Woodstock* soundtrack. Could you tell me some more about that, if indeed there is more to tell . . . ?'

In that they existed at all Teenagers in Trouble were a band that dwelt in the imagination of my friend James Webster and I. Together we ran a small record label called Planet Records, the offices of which consisted of a table and filing cabinet propped up against a wall in the Revolver back room. We had released a series of 7" singles by bands mainly from Bristol, and Teenagers In Trouble were our conception of the perfect group. As such conceptions usually originated around last orders, we had decided that the first Teenagers in Trouble release would be a limited edition cassette-only cover version of the entire *Woodstock* soundtrack, and that Webster and I would be the band's core members. Such was our confidence in the project that we had written a brief overview of the release and had assigned it a catalogue number in our latest Planet Records fact sheet. These took the form of a small typed insert written in a semi-confrontational house style, included with every single.

Although flattered and excited that this act of small-hours absurdism had prompted a phone call from John Peel, I also wondered how I might temper his interest by informing him that Teenagers In Trouble were not yet ready to record their tribute and were largely, in fact entirely, a product of pub table fantasy.

Before I could clarify that the band's modus operandi was in its infancy and still something of an abstraction Peel further expanded on the reasons for his call.

'In their wisdom the BBC have decided that Radio 1 should celebrate the twenty-fifth anniversary of Woodstock. I can't really offer any explanation as to why they have come to this decision, but I thought for my programme at least, perhaps Teenagers In Trouble were the very band for this job?'

'Well,' I said. 'We, I mean they . . . they're a little unpredictable, but I could send you a tape of what they might consider suitable for broadcast.'

A few weeks later Webster and I had convened in a quiet side street pub on a balmy August Friday night. We were far too anxious to listen to the John Peel show that evening. Instead we placed ourselves in the corner of the back room and desperately attempted to avoid any discussion of whether the cassette we had sent the DJ might be played during that night's broadcast.

The following day we shared an emotion familiar to the infinite number of John Peel listeners who had been transformed from being members of the programme's audience to one of its performers; a transformation that had been instigated solely by the curiosity and benevolence of the DJ. A friend had recorded the show and the following morning had dropped a cassette off at the Revolver counter. I chose a quiet moment when the shop was empty to try and overcome my unease and play the tape. I remained astonished by the fact that Peel had been kind enough to broadcast the recordings of myself and Webster improvising and free-associating in my kitchen. As Peel began his introduction he explained that rather than the usual session, that night's programme would consist of four cover versions of the *Woodstock* soundtrack specially recorded in Bristol 'by our friends Teenagers In Trouble'.

On a cold morning six months later I was once again in deep telephone conversation with the DJ. Peel had rung to inform us that Radio 1 were hosting that year's Sound City, their annual week of live regional broadcasts in

Bristol. 'And,' he continued, 'the budget cuts are currently so draconian that I may well have to ask if I might kip on your floor.'

In the intervening period between the forthcoming Sound City and Teenagers In Trouble's debut appearance on national radio, Webster and I had released a further handful of 7" singles. Each release had sold reasonably well and in my exuberance I convinced myself that this was due to the cultivated air of outsider resistance we felt Planet Records represented in the contemporary independent music landscape. A few years later I realised, with only a little reflection, that any success we achieved (success which plainly needed to be qualified) was largely due to the patronage of John Peel.

The spring had come early and by April the redeveloped docks of the city had begun their annual metamorphosis into a free-spirited if sedate waterfront.

I had arranged to meet Peel at Revolver on the Tuesday morning of Radio 1's week-long residency, having informed him that from there we would make our way to the docks in time for the start of the Planet Records boat trip. The pretext for this pleasant excursion around the harbour, if indeed any existed, had been a conversation between Webster and me that had centred on the need to stage some form of intervention against the BBC's highly conventional programming.

I loitered along the shop corridor in anticipation of John

Peel's arrival, and before he had taken a few steps through the doorway I hurriedly made my introductions and led him towards my nearby car. Within a few moments we were driving down Park Street as Peel settled into the passenger seat and began surveying the contents around him.

'Empty tape boxes and the odd flyer for a Tuesday night. I have to say this is not an unfamiliar environment,' he said.

As we passed through the city to the docks I listened as Peel spoke with little pause throughout our journey. He moved between topics but lingered on the subject of his family. His father had been an officer during the Second World War and was largely absent during his early childhood. One day a figure on a motorcycle arrived at the house where Peel and his family were spending their summer holiday in north Wales.

'I was around six years old,' Peel continued, 'and the sudden realisation that this man was my father meant that I was finding it hard to breathe. I had this extraordinary physical reaction.' Once he had described his childhood the DJ mentioned that his current familial affairs were becoming increasingly convoluted. 'One of our daughters has a boyfriend who occasionally gets into trouble. And one of our neighbours is a Justice of the Peace, so my daughter's boyfriend occasionally has to leave through the back door . . .'

Our journey had lasted a little over twenty minutes. As we left the car and walked towards the marina, I realised we hadn't once spoken about music.

The sailing conditions were fine and an ad hoc bar had been constructed on board our chartered sight-seeing boat. Around thirty of us set sail for a tour around the harbour and some friends who had set up their equipment in the prow started playing a loud drone.

After half an hour or so the drone had grown in volume and listening to it felt a little more visceral. The boat was now out into the middle course of the River Avon where the wind had picked up. The white noise of the river and the undulating movements of the hull cutting through the water combined with the frequencies of the droning feedback to create a hypnotic sense of calm. I looked around and although many of them had pulled their collars up against the breeze, all aboard were smiling. I walked towards Peel, who had spent the voyage in benign conversation with his fellow passengers, and asked him what he thought of the music.

'The perfect accompaniment to the afternoon's sight-seeing,' he assured me and in as undemonstrative a manner as possible he lightly raised a plastic tumbler with a smile.

That evening Planet Records was hosting a series of performances as part of the official Sound City fringe at the Louisiana, a pub located reasonably near a basin on the Avon.

I had asked the captain if we could disembark as near as possible to the venue, as the thought of us carrying our equipment up from the moorings and on to the stage had seemed noteworthy enough. As I walked along the jetty I realised that an afternoon spent drinking red wine on the river's lively currents had ensured that I would be spending the rest of the evening on my sea legs.

The following afternoon John Peel wondered up to the Revolver counter and asked if David Pearce of Flying Saucer Attack and myself would like to accompany him for a cup of afternoon tea.

We spent the following few hours in the wholefood café that was annexed to a Steiner school a short uphill walk from Revolver. There Peel shared with us stories from his life and career: about how in his early twenties, while working as a clerk at an insurance company in Texas, he had stood a few yards from Lee Harvey Oswald as he was shot, how his first marriage had been so difficult and dramatic that he had felt ill-equipped to deal with its consequences and how in the Faces he had found a band whose performances had liberated him from many of his anxieties.

As he told us the full story of his appearance as a mandolin player with the Faces and Rod Stewart on *Top of the Pops* his voice cracked a little. With a slight halting he began to share another story about Rod Stewart at the BBC Television Centre.

'This was a few years later,' he said, 'and Rod was by now a superstar. He was recording a show at the BBC Theatre and I mentioned to him beforehand that my niece was in the audience, sitting in the front row, and that she was not just an enormous fan, but absolutely enthralled to be there.

I asked Rod if he might give her a wave if I pointed her out to him, but instead . . .' and here his voice changed from its familiar lugubriousness to a hesitant burr '. . . instead he sang an entire song to her while holding her hand, he really was an absolute gentleman, I have to say.'

On the final day of Sound City Peel was to broadcast his programme live from BBC Radio Bristol on a Saturday afternoon. We had once again arranged to meet in Revolver and as I walked through the doorway I saw Roger and the DJ deep in conversation and noted that Roger had his arms folded, a gesture that often meant he was both literally and figuratively standing his ground.

Peel turned towards me with just a hint of strain in his features.

'We're trying to establish whether you have had the latest Johnny Hash single on In the Red,' he said, 'but at the moment we're a little in the dark.'

Before I could reply Roger shrugged his shoulders and with mild assertion began speaking over Peel's head.

'We can try ordering them for you, if you like. We'll send it on.'

Sensing their exchange had reached an impasse, I asked Peel if he would accompany me into the back room. I pointed towards a shabby unlit corner. 'Before we head to the studio I just wanted to show you this,' I said, and opened the Revolver lavatory door.

Peel regarded me with hesitation but his ever-present air

of benevolence remained. As our eyes adjusted to the light, I indicated the reason for our visit to one of the shop's least hospitable alcoves and I watched as the smile broadened on the DJ's face.

'I really don't remember doing that at all,' he said. 'Is there a date?'

In large capitals someone had once written:

LIVERPOOL THE GODS ARE ON THE MARCH AGAIN

Underneath this assertion had been written a rejoinder in a tightly wound hand:

Unfortunately in the wrong direction

Below this its author had placed his signature:

John Peel

'No, there's no date,' I said, delighted that I had been able to show Peel his handiwork and delighted as well to place Revolver in an historical context.

As we drove the half a mile towards the BBC studios, I thought it polite to mention that Roger's ability to produce a frisson in any potential customer was an attribute that he shared with everyone who walked towards the counter.

'He's been selling records just like that all his life,' I said.

'Yes,' Peel replied immediately. 'Perhaps for a little too long. It may be time for a change of career.'

During that afternoon's broadcast Peel played music by Flying Saucer Attack and Movietone and invited Webster and myself into the studio as live guests. At one point he asked us how we made a living apart from running Planet Records.

'We hustle,' Webster replied without hesitation.

'A not unattractive way of putting it,' Peel answered and then introduced the next record.

We remained in the studio for the duration of the second hour of the programme. At one point his production assistant, Alison Howe, came into the studio and whispered into his ear.

A fortnight earlier I had made arrangements for appearing on the programme with the show's producer, who, I now realised, was absent from the current broadcast.

When I had briefly met him earlier in the week, this producer had been wearing matching jeans and denim jacket. In my imagination, anyone in a position of authority at the John Peel Show would have had characteristics similar to those of John Walters, the programme's hirsute and garrulous gatekeeper for much of the 1970s and '80s, a man who had often worn a sports jacket and tie to watch punk bands play at the Vortex. The current producer with whom I had a passing conversation had cut a far less prepossessing figure.

I felt emboldened by the activities and conversations of the preceding few days. I was also feeling relaxed by an hour spent in one of the BBC's high-backed leather chairs, to such an extent I found myself asking Peel whether his producer would be attending.

'No, he won't,' he replied, peering over his glasses, which along with his headphones made him suddenly look like an authoritative broadcasting professional.

'Earlier in the week it was decided that there wasn't quite enough room in the BBC for both of us,' he continued, 'and here I am.'

Howe once again leant over to talk quietly to Peel. Webster and I began our own conversation, one that quickly trailed off. In the pause before our on-air discourse began again, I was struck by what Peel had said and the manner in which he had spoken. To have endured for so long at Radio 1 he must have had to tolerate innumerable changes of policy and personnel, I thought, but rather than dismiss them as specious or irrelevant he has learned to adapt and survive. His abiding capacity to discover new music had remained undisputed over the decades, and I now realised that it was this rare ability that had ensured he could invariably place himself above the realpolitik of the BBC and its infatuation with demographics. Over tea a day or so before he had told me that he consistently attracted the youngest audience on national radio and as he did so his face had flushed with uncharacteristic pride.

The reason for the whispered conversations between Peel and the production assistant became clear. Towards the end of the programme, while resolutely staring down at the studio controls in front of him, he raised his right arm and gave a brisk but deliberate wave, a gesture he appeared to be making under duress.

As surreptitiously as possible I turned around in an attempt to see who had been the subject of this rather forced greeting. For a moment I wondered if the newly discarded producer had decided to make one final studio appearance in an act of atonement or perhaps even in a moment of antagonism.

Instead of the matching denims of the ex-producer, I saw a rather bedraggled figure, one I had noticed as we had entered the building and who must have been sitting in reception for the duration of the programme.

He was positioned on a chair at the far end of the room, which meant that he was just visible through the control room and had been able to watch the broadcast. A man in his mid-twenties, with rather lank hair and a look of extreme concentration on his face, the figure became animated with an endearing clumsiness when he saw that the DJ had been waving in his direction.

As the programme ended and we thanked Peel for his generosity, I asked Howe who the figure in reception had been.

'He's from Estonia,' she explained, 'and listens religiously.

I'm not sure how. I think it's through his computer but I haven't worked it out. There are hundreds of them listening every week, probably more, and they come on these pilgrimages from all over to see John.'

The week had left me simultaneously dazed and over-stimulated. As Webster and I started walking towards a pub in silence, I could feel my energy dwindling with every step. The events of the past few days were competing with each other for my attention but each remembered moment was interrupted by the vision of John Peel waving at the Estonian pilgrim sitting in reception. I found it hard to reconcile the DJ who had looked down awkwardly at his console, while forcing himself to give a wave, with the patient, affable, warm man who had been so generous with his companionship throughout the week. A thought struck me and gradually I felt as though I was beginning to understand why Peel had been so shy and reluctant to engage with his attentive and well-travelled listener.

Anyone involved in music that I had met through Revolver or through my attempts at running a small record company seemed to share an awkwardness. Although the shop was often the location and starting point for animated conversation, if the subject ever deviated from music, little was shared or discussed with the same levels of enthusiasm or articulacy.

Throughout his career Peel had surrounded himself with such people, people who had taken a decision to devote themselves to the margins, a place from where they inevitably found themselves in regular correspondence with the DJ. He developed an instinct for nurturing the talent and desires in anyone who had surrendered to music, irrespective of the genre in which they were immersed. Gabba, dancehall, techno, dub or the rickety guitar songs that followed punk and with which he became over identified, Peel had faith in anyone in whose music he heard an uncontrollable compulsion. But perhaps outside the comfort of such margins he was as shy and bewildered as the rest of us who sought sanctuary in the fringes of creativity and was as self-effacing and unconfident as the Sea Urchins or the founders of Sarah Records. Peel had spent a lifetime receiving demos, letters and self-released singles from awkward and over-attentive listeners and aspirant musicians, but the fan that had travelled from Estonia merely to observe him at work rather than to ask him to share in any such pathologies left John Peel bewildered and introverted.

8

Nine months after listening to him talk so discursively and warm-heartedly about Rod Stewart, the memories of the afternoon spent with John Peel were suddenly flooding my consciousness. I was attempting to remember an anecdote he had told about the singer in his formative years and in doing so, hoped that it would make sense of the unfamiliar state in which I suddenly found myself.

Earlier that morning I had answered the phone in Revolver, assuming it would be the usual call from someone working in telesales for a distributor who wanted to pitch us their new releases. Instead I had been informed that my friend Joshua Compston, someone whom I had known since school, had died.

On hearing of his death I had immediately left the shop and walked towards home. Once there I felt an overwhelming urge for company and, if not conversation, then the familiar Revolver atmosphere of stalled time.

As I turned back towards to the shop, an item that I had previously regarded as a typical piece of back-room detritus suddenly gained a totemic significance. Upon my arrival I was determined to locate a tatty and battered cassette cover, the contents of which were missing but, it was assumed, might one day reappear in one of the shop's dusty corners like a bad penny. The cassette in question was *Every Picture Tells a Story*, the third solo Rod Stewart album, on which 'Maggie May' on side two had established the singer as an international rock star. It was a record I knew intimately, so much so that in my current heightened state I could recall every missed beat, hesitant vocal line or broken note that gave the record its tumbledown charm.

Five years earlier the album had been the sole musical accompaniment to a long week spent hitchhiking from London to southern France. It was a journey I had undertaken with Joshua.

At school Joshua had cut a unique figure. He was fond of testing the patience of those around him and was fearless in his attempts at promoting his sense of individuality, a task he outwardly maintained by wearing second hand tweeds and waistcoats and having his wavy blond hair cut in the style of George Orwell.

Joshua had once walked around the school quad with a cross on his back and explained that, as he was taking divinity A level, it was necessary for him to research the physiological experiences of Christ. Weeks later he was once again reprimanded; the new offence had been to wear a master's gown to lessons. Joshua had protested that the wearing of gowns by pupils was neither included in nor prohibited by the school rules. Such was the frequency and originality with which he tested the school's patience that it was decided that Joshua would be granted the rare privilege of being allowed to be a weekly boarder.

Every weekend Joshua returned to the home in Strand-on-the Green near Kew Bridge in south-west London that he and his sister shared with their mother and stepfather. The house lay behind a small walled garden and was barely visible from the road. An anonymous door in the wall opened on to a yard full of disparate objects and sculptures surrounding a path that ran downwards to a nineteenth-century brick house overlooking the Thames. Although not grand in the manner of many of the houses that line the river as it flows westwards towards Richmond and Surrey, the atmosphere of Joshua's family home was as distinctive as its architecture.

I was thinking of the floor-to-ceiling glass windows either side of the door to Joshua's house as I walked back to Revolver, and how their length allowed both parties standing at it, the visitor and the occupant, to see each other before they were able to speak. On my route to the shop was a small café that I occasionally visited to break my short daily walk. I rarely drank tea but remembered that it was often recommended to people experiencing shock. There was a table near the entrance with a view of the street. From a bench I stared at the everyday activities and traffic that seemed to meander in front of me. I attempted to collect myself before the proprietor came to take my order but suddenly felt overwhelmed by a force that age teaches us are the unimpeded currents of grief. Copies of that morning's newspapers lay near the café window. I picked one or two from the small pile and, as I glanced through them, I began weeping without any regard for what anyone there might think. One of the newspapers, the *Independent*, carried a picture of Joshua on the cover of its supplement section. It had been taken at 'The Hanging Picnic', a happening-cum-al fresco tea party that he had instigated the previous summer in Hoxton Square, and for which he had co-ordinated a 'picnic committee' to encourage artists to exhibit their work on the square's railings. The photograph showed Joshua in a white, collarless cocktail waiter's suit standing in the middle of the crowd that had gathered to participate.

In the instant of being aware of his death, I had immediately run through my memory attempting to locate the last occasion that I had seen Joshua. It had been in a Wandsworth pub a few months earlier, when he had seemed deflated and, as was his way when subdued, rather confrontational. There were various tics and gestures Joshua would use to alleviate the atmosphere whenever he felt low. At school he would eat apples in their entirety while insisting that he enjoyed the core; in the evenings after lessons he would often wander around in brown smocks or overalls as a tribute to William Morris and Eric Gill and also in order to differentiate himself from us, his schoolboy peers. He also insisted on walking everywhere at a ridiculous and disconcerting pace, as if to provoke anyone walking alongside him to demand that he slow down.

The gesture I most associated with his darker moods was the slow, rather angry, removal of his glasses. He would then blow on the lenses and rub them with a handkerchief. This was a long process undertaken with a mannered deliberation. As he did so, Joshua fixed the onlooker with a glare of mock piety that would, depending on the recipient's reaction, eventually turn into a self-deprecating smile. In company, at least, Joshua was usually capable of transforming his melancholy into an engaging spectacle.

Before he had turned eighteen Joshua had a thorough knowledge of art history, especially from the late nineteenth century onwards. Rather than their work, it was the unstructured stubbornness of artists' lives with which he most identified. In *Leap into the Void* the French artist Yves Klein presented an image of himself falling from a building in mid-air, as if ecstatic about the possibility of colliding with the pavement below. Joshua often referred to Klein's work when insisting that gestures and interventions were of more significance than life drawing or brushwork to his idea of a new, expansionist form of contemporary art. He had also developed an eye for discarded objects that he often found while rummaging in skips or that he haggled for in junk shops. Anything of value, such as objects made of Bakelite, he would then sell to one or other of the stallholders he had cultivated on Portobello Market during his weekly return to London.

For his art A level Joshua filled a hamster cage with rusty detritus and industrial ephemera such as bolts and screws. On the base of the cage he wrote a statement in the form of a provocative question in his distinct and childish hand – he hadn't learned to write until quite late into infancy:

These objects are trapped. Are you trapped?

This object was installed on a plinth for the summer Gaudy, an occasion when parents were invited into the art block to inspect recent work by the sixth form. Allowed pride of place alongside the customary still-lifes of cut flowers and studio ceramics, Joshua's installation drew a great deal of attention from its viewers, some of it rather concerned; at times the reaction approached hostility.

The prominence of Joshua's work in the exhibition was a reminder that although he tested their leniency, the school admired and respected the imagination with which he attempted to exert his will.

A weekend spent away from school with Joshua usually involved a trip on the river.

On the banks on the Thames a few steps in front of his the family's house in London was moored a small wooden yellow dinghy. At the top of the hull small strips of blue water-resistant tape had been affixed to form the letters: B U S B Y S – O – G, (the hyphenated S-O-G being an acronym of Strand-on-the-Green).

Joshua made a great play of carrying a heavy outboard engine from the house to fit to the boat's stern. As he did so he would bark instructions about who should sit where and who was in charge of which oar. After pulling the start cord with marked fervour, an action that became histrionic if there were girls present, Joshua would begin to steer the boat upstream as the propeller created a gentle wake. Once the course had been settled he would press 'play' on a battered tape player, one so decrepit that its front casing was missing. We would smoke a joint and watch as the lights along the Thames grew brighter and the chill headwind, in the manner only ever experienced during adolescence, felt both stimulating and comforting. Joshua's then girlfriend was a year or so older than him and had developed a fascination with Syd Barrett while waiting to take up a place at art school. I first heard 'Arnold Layne', 'Remember A Day' and the other psychedelic Pink Floyd songs above the sound of the boat's engine as our clothes grew damp from the spray and we sat in stoned silence looking out across the encroaching darkness of the murky Thames.

After one such trip in the autumn of 1987 we hurriedly changed into dry clothes and took the tube from Gunnersbury into the West End. I felt increasingly self-conscious as we approached Oxford Circus. I was wearing one of Joshua's tweed jackets and a tie that he had picked out for me from the large tallboy in his bedroom; he had decided upon an outfit of plus fours and a matching hacking jacket. That year the journalist and television presenter Daniel Farson had published *Soho in the Fifties* a memoir of his dissolute experiences spent stumbling through the area. The book featured pictures from the archive of the photographer John Deakin: images of choleric painters, muses, sailors and various roués to whom Joshua had developed an emotional attachment. He also held the book's anecdotes of alcoholic lunchtimes spent eating oysters that led to desiccated afternoons collapsed on the floors of artists' studios in the highest regard.

Inspired by Deakin's photographs we had travelled to the West End with the intention of spending the evening in the Colony Room, a private club on Dean Street that had featured in Farson's book; it had been one of the few establishments in London licensed for daytime drinking. Our clothes had been chosen in an attempt at integration into what we imagined was a typical Saturday night Colony ~~~d to lend us the air of seasoned Soho habitués. In reality ou costumes merely accentuated the fact we were under age, something that was doubtless a pressing concern in a member's club, particularly one renowned for disreputable behaviour.

We crossed Dean Street and wandered down towards the dead end of Richmond Mews, where we quickly drank two cans of beer each in the hope that we might feel emboldened to make our entrance. Back on Dean Street we stepped briskly along the innocuous passageway that led from the pavement to the small green door above which was the sign that read 'Colony Room Club 1st Floor' and in smaller letters 'MEMBERS ONLY'.

Once we had walked through this entrance and up a narrow flight of stairs we encountered another door; Joshua pushed it open without hesitation. The dense smoke and high levels of noise inside the club immediately disorientated me but Joshua attempted to reach the bar by politely forcing our way through a small animated group that had assembled near the door. We were immediately noticed and became, in an instant, the subjects of gesticulation and abuse. I turned around and quickly ran down the stairs, feeling nauseous as the mixture of adrenaline and light-headedness from our swiftly consumed beer forced me to lean against the wall on the ground floor. Joshua was being man-handled and only managed to avoid being thrown down the stairs by waving his arms aggressively at his captors, one of whom kicked Joshua's backside in retaliation, a blow that sent him to the bottom step.

As we slowly made our way down Dean Street and began to lick our wounds, Joshua assured me that he would one day become a member of the Colony and use the evening's confrontation as leverage with which to hasten the processing of his application.

*

After leaving school Joshua took a foundation course at Camberwell School of Art, where he sought the friendship of anyone who understood the significance that the school included among its alumni Syd Barrett. He then completed a degree at the Courtauld Institute where, having only partially convinced the authorities of its necessity, he curated an exhibition in the institute's study rooms and lecture theatres. The exhibition included work by Howard Hodgkin and Gilbert & George along with emerging contemporary artists such as Langlands & Bell, Fiona Rae, Damien Hirst and Gary Hume, and was judged to be a great success. The exhibition brought Joshua his first broadsheet notices and the start of an enduring friendship with Gilbert & George whom Joshua had located by scouring the cafés off Brick Lane.

Artists began to feature prominently in Joshua's life. At his twenty-first birthday party at Strand-on-the-Green Peter Blake arrived with a painting under his arm that he gave to Joshua, along with birthday greetings spoken in his rather baleful voice.

Once he had graduated from the Courtauld Joshua intended to open a gallery in the East End. He had informed me of his plans the preceding year while we sat, shivering slightly on the grass bank of a *route nationale* as we waited for the morning sun to dry the dew that had collected on our backs overnight. It was late July in the mid-west of France and that morning we were hoping for a lift from a camion that might take us further south towards Uzès, where Joshua's stepmother had part-ownership of a cottage. While assessing our chances of reaching our destination that day Joshua reached for the same tape recorder that had accompanied us on the boat trips along the Thames. He pressed the battered 'play' button and after a few bars of forcefully plucked guitar and mandolin, the voice of Rod Stewart, now accompanied by a drum beat that appeared to be composed entirely of belligerent tom-tom fills, echoed out across the Auvergne countryside.

Had I known Joshua intended to bring the cassette player on our journey I would have ensured that the provision of tapes fell under my jurisdiction. As we had embarked on our journey I had tried, with some difficulty, to disguise my consternation at the thought that the soundtrack to our longs days ahead spent loitering in lay-bys was to be a Rod Stewart solo album.

At school, much to the amusement of many of my friends, I had developed the habit of scouring the music papers every Wednesday. I especially enjoyed interviews with musicians such as Peter Buck, who turned his dialogue with journalists into a form of quasi-canonical name-dropping. When asked about a new release by his band R.E.M. he would list the influences on its creation as though reading out the imaginary index of his record collection. Buck had accumulated boxes of vinyl and an attendant working knowledge of B sides and lost recordings while working in a record shop, Wuxtry Records in the band's hometown of Athens, Georgia. There he had developed a taste for half-forgotten, introspective records from the early 1970s. By reading his interviews I had discovered artists such as Big Star, Tim Buckley and Nick Drake. However, as their catalogues were either deleted or only to be found in specialist shops and market stalls in London, I had so far only heard them as second-generation tapes. Although I remembered the Faces being mentioned in a live review of a London concert by the Replacements, I had no memory of Rod Stewart's solo records being regarded with any form of reverence, let alone the kind of hallowed approval bestowed on albums from the era by Peter Buck.

Joshua was certainly interested in music but he thought behaviour such as reading the music weeklies was inane. As he set off at an aggressively brisk pace, even by his standards, towards New Covent Garden Market, where we intended to secure our cross-Channel lift, he suddenly gripped the tape player with renewed authority as if it were an attaché case. I began to wonder if Joshua, assuming the thought had even crossed his mind, had brought this Rod Stewart tape on our journey solely for his amusement.

Stewart had recorded *Every Picture Tells a Story* in the same manner in which he had made his first two solo albums, quickly and with an anonymous studio band that was accustomed to recording late at night and completing a song in no more than two or three takes. Stewart's solo career was maintained in tandem with his position as the lead singer and front man for the Faces. He consequently treated his solo records with even less formality than those by his band. On his first four solo records Stewart credited himself as their producer and recorded a series of albums that emphasised his love of American R'n'B and Bob Dylan. Stewart also included a few compositions of his own that were usually co-written, songs that were often notable for lyrics based on internal rhymes and lack of a chorus. The sound on these records was rustic and carefree and strewn with yelps, fluffed lines, missed cues and loose drum beats suggestive of an atmosphere in which the good times had rolled, almost to the point of indifference towards the finished recording. With his rasping voice set among acoustic guitars, fiddles and mandolins over which he frequently dispensed cowboy whoops and hollers, Stewart presented himself as an unlikely hybrid of Tom Sawyer and Jack the Lad.

The unpretentious manner in which he approached his solo work was evident in Stewart's sleeve notes. On the back cover of *Every Picture Tells a Story* Martin Quittenton, the bespectacled and introspective acoustic guitarist who co-wrote 'Maggie May' with the singer, was billed as 'Martell Brandy Martin Quittenton' while Stewart's co-vocalist on two songs, Madeleine Bell, was given the prefix 'Mateus Rose'. The sense that inebriation was unconditional was evident in the credits the singer gave to the musician who played the instrument that had given the album, and 'Maggie May' in particular, its distinctive sound:

> The mandolin was played by the mandolin player in Lindisfarne – the name slips my mind.

There may have been contractual reasons for Stewart's evasiveness but such unaffected wit added to the record's air of approachability.

This inclusive, everyman style reaches its apotheosis on Stewart's fourth solo album *Never A Dull Moment*. On the inner gatefold photograph the singer, musicians and studio engineers are photographed between two goal posts, standing or kneeling along the goal line. Stewart, who is wearing a tartan scarf and matching Tam O'Shanter, is leaning against one of the posts, which is badly chipped and marked. The wire fence that can be seen at the rear of the goal, the privet hedges and uniform mid-century housing in the background, the condition of the goal and the scrubby overgrown grass of the pitch all indicate the shared enjoyment of a municipal playing field. The names of the musicians and recording personnel are printed in capitals on the cross bar and written in the unaffected vernacular of a Sunday league team sheet. Stewart lists himself as 'STEWARTY', standing next to him in a polo ˡˑ is the suitably stoical-looking Martin Quittenton who ˑˑfully credited by surname rather than nickname.

Ronnie Lane of the Faces is 'LANEOLE' and Ronnie Wood, unequivocally known to the early 1970s rock cognoscenti and beyond as 'Woody', and who is seen wearing the kind of eye mask usually associated with transatlantic air travel, is labelled 'WOODSY'. The list continues along the bar and includes names as diverse and inconsequential as 'Groundstaff', 'Person', 'Brian' and 'Tricky Dicky'. The pianist Pete Sears is absent but represented by a football until finally, covering the right-hand goal post, Stewart has written a tribute to the band members missing from the photograph:

IAN MCLAGAN & KENNEY JONES DECIDED TO STAY IN BED

Many of those present in the photograph are unsurprisingly wearing broad grins.

A similar infectiousness could be heard on Stewart's records. Four minutes into the title track of *Every Picture Tells a Story*, one of the musicians, possibly a highly committed Ronnie Wood, elicits a softly delivered and spontaneous 'Hey!', an interjection of rapt delight at participating in the song's creation. As we crossed France, idling for hours while waiting for a benevolent HGV, Joshua and I would listen out for this exclamation over and over again.

Along with 'Maggie May' and the title track, Stewart had written the album's most affecting song, 'Mandolin Wind'. For this number the singer imagined himself as a frontiersman looking out over the prairie while declaring love for the sweetheart with whom he had made it through the 'coldest winter in almost forty years', unlike the herd of buffalo that had been unable to survive the freezing conditions of the plains.

However unlikely or preposterous this scenario, Stewart, accompanied by the suggestive lilt of a mandolin, sang with an impassioned conviction that gave the song an undeniable emotional pull.

On the night we spent on the roadside verge before waking dew-laden the next morning, Joshua and I had drunk enough wine to knock ourselves out for an evening under the stars. We had undoubtedly felt its effects as Joshua turned towards me and raised his head with an exaggerated seriousness.

'It's time more people tried to live their lives like Rod Stewart,' he told me, although his words were a little slurred.

'If they did then the world would be a far better place.'

*

That winter on a dank and miserable early December day Joshua and I were the only people present in the Colony Room, other than its proprietor Ian Board. Since the night ⌐e had been ejected ignominiously via the club's staircase, ⌐ taken Joshua a little over two years to become a ⌐ privilege he had been granted as an eighteenth-birthday present, although on such a dreary day it was an achievement that seemed futile. The paintings, framed photographs and other antediluvian clutter that hung on the Colony's dark green walls were barely visible in the stale, toxic air.

Although it was customary for him to appear dishevelled, Board appeared to be in an advanced stage of listlessness; his large, disfigured nose had the colour and texture of a rusted standpipe. For all the hedonism associated with Old Soho, at that moment there was a sense of nihilism about the club. As the smoke from Joshua and Board's cigarettes hung suspended in the atmosphere, the cramped space suggested a closed ward rather than a room maintained for prestigious alcoholic decadence.

Board sat in his usual position, which allowed him to keep one eye on the door while his left elbow remained supported by the bar. There, as Joshua and I settled on the green banquettes that ran either side of one of the club's corners, he maintained the authoritative silence of a person negotiating their way through the labyrinths of too much afternoon gin, a silence that was as perceptible as the cigarette smoke.

Joshua understood the members' unwritten protocol attached to such fugues and busied himself in the Gladstone bag that he used as a briefcase.

At an attempt at conviviality, or to at least show that I was not intimidated by his coiled-spring posture and reputation for an acidic tongue, I decided to engage Board in conversation and said the first thing that came into my mind.

'Are you doing anything for Christmas?' I asked.

'Ooh,' said Board instantly, without changing his gaze towards the counter. 'I expect I shall have a wank.'

Although Joshua had been pretending to search for some elusive item in his bag while I attempted to talk to Board, he could not prevent himself from emitting a high-pitched laugh. At that moment we were joined in the dying daylight of the Colony Room by one of its regulars.

'Hello Frances,' said Board with a coy smile.

'Champagne! Hello . . .' replied Frances Bacon.

Without pause Joshua had resumed looking through the contents of his doctor's bag and produced a battered-looking pamphlet that he now waved at the artist sternly.

'Look at this,' said Joshua as he encouraged Bacon to join us on the banquettes.

'It's from the First World War, an original copy, "The Effects of Mustard Gas on the Battle Field and Their Proprietary Uses, with Illustrations".'

'How extrao-o-ordinary,' Bacon smiled as he waved towards Board again.

'Champagne!'

On a silver tray Board had placed four glasses of champagne each containing a swizzle stick.

'All those years they put the bubbles in and then you –

Frances – insist on taking them all out,' said Board, now animated to the point where his elbows were making involuntary movements as if in accompaniment to his raised voice. In response, Bacon let out a hoarse cough and appeared to double up in laughter.

I was struck that despite his reputation as someone whose withering and vituperative tongue had often brought people to tears of either laughter or shamefaced sorrow, Ian Board was as capable of anodyne saloon bar banter as any careworn licensee. Or perhaps I was drawing the wrong conclusion, and that rather than witnessing a routine commonplace to any golf or Rotary club, the Colony Room host and its most venerated member were engaged in a brief satirical double act that signalled the beginning of a long evening's drinking. As I felt the soothing effects of the champagne, whatever the reasons for their routine I thought, any distinctions have long vanished.

Frances Bacon and Joshua were looking intently at the early chemical warfare treatment manual, although Bacon seemed to be acting out of weary politeness, or out of a general curiosity about Joshua, rather than in any interest in the contents of the pamphlet.

'The tones on these faces, these purples – look at the bruised green around his eyes,' said Joshua assertively with cigarette in hand 'It's as if colour is being used to frighten the person consulting this manual into taking action.'

Board had started topping up our glasses. Bacon looked

up from the manual towards Joshua. He flickered for a few seconds, caught in the momentary realisation that he was being given a tutorial by a twenty-one-year-old. He gave Joshua a benign sigh along with a bewildered half glance and cautiously made his way to the bar with a newfound steadiness and once there, he gripped its Formica top in gratitude of its familiar reassurance.

Joshua opened a gallery in 1992, as had been his intention. It was situated in a former print works on Charlotte Road, off Old Street in Hoxton, an area that was then considered a hinterland by the Cork Street art establishment. Rather than name the gallery after himself as was the Mayfair convention, or use the location or former use of the premises as inspiration, Joshua named his gallery Factual Nonsense, often shortened to FN, a phrase he attributed to Wittgenstein and an acronym that suggested a movement or what is now known as a brand. There was an elegant symmetry to the words and to the equivalence in their number of letters, something that was accentuated by the deep red colour Joshua utilised for the gallery name on all its letterheads, posters and other printed material. If they were spoken together in the same sentence Factual Nonsense and its proprietor's name could give the impression of a burgeoning art movement, an impression that Joshua longed to create.

At the northern end of Charlotte Road was a minicab office. At night its low-wattage bulbs illuminated a small stretch of the pavement on Old Street that otherwise felt deserted apart from the liveliness of the London Apprentice a few steps further along the road. Factual Nonsense was located at the other end of the road, towards Great Eastern Street. On weekends there was the occasional thud of a sound system and the intermittent flashing of lights from basements on the streets nearby, but other than the contained and muted sound of parties there was a stillness surrounding Joshua's gallery. I would sometimes meet him in his two nearest pubs, the Bricklayers Arms or the Barley Mow, where he seemed to be on speaking terms with many of the clientele. The people Joshua introduced me to in the pubs – other than their landlords – often described themselves as artists. The conversations I overheard between them tended to concern forthcoming events and I sensed that although Joshua was speaking to people who seemed enthusiastic about his ideas, they also appeared preoccupied. I remember feeling relieved that nearly everyone in his immediate surroundings gave the impression that they took Joshua seriously.

One morning I awoke in a sleeping bag on the Factual Nonsense floor as the scent of tobacco wafted from the partition at the back of the gallery where Joshua slept, and began to permeate the building. His bed was a specially constructed platform; this, together with a dark wooden plan chest and antique desk, created a similar atmosphere to that of his study at school and his bedroom at Strand-on-the-Green. During gallery hours there would often be a friend, girlfriend or assistant acting as a gallery manager, who, with tireless concentration, watched Joshua outlining his thoughts on whichever project was in planning.

I stared at the white gallery walls hung with paintings and works on paper and was reminded that Joshua had told me, as he had most of his school friends, that we would one day awake on his gallery floor.

I could hear his early morning hacking cough and remembered that late into the previous night he had offered me his uncharacteristic congratulations for having had music played on the John Peel programme; for a moment I felt as though all the schoolboy daydreams we had shared about our future were growing tangible.

My next visit to Factual Nonsense revealed signs that problems were developing. Joshua and I were deep in conversation when a suited man, carrying a brief case with the distinctive insignia of a Customs and Excise civil servant, walked through the gallery and asked Joshua to confirm that his surname was Compston. I wandered towards the other side of the room and would have made a careful inspection of the exhibition had the walls not been bare. Joshua had told me that he was between shows but I wondered if he was running into difficulties. As he dealt with this visit from the tax man, Joshua's manner was scrupulous. I noticed that he had also lowered his voice to the unwavering RP register he occasionally used in public or if he felt he was being underestimated.

Whenever Factual Nonsense was hosting an opening or Joshua was at large in East London he maintained his presence as an art-world entryist, fixer and impresario.

He arranged drinks sponsorship for the closing party of Sarah Lucas and Tracey Emin's shop in Bethnal Green and hosted the Fete Worse Than Death street parties that, along with the later FN Party Conference and Hanging Picnic became synonymous with the re-invention of Hoxton as a new form of urban artistic community. Occasionally Joshua would put on a laboured cockney accent as he described these events or parties as 'a knees up, mate, proper knees up'.

I wondered if he spoke that way because he was increasingly self-possessed, or perhaps, the further he went into his grand project for the East End, the more detached he became, oblivious to his surroundings.

The first Fete Worse Than Death featured a kissing booth run by Tracey Emin, Damien Hirst and Gary Hume dressed as circus clowns; one of them, in a gesture appropriate to the location, called himself 'I Should Coco the Clown'. The Factual Nonsense letterpress-and-cartridge-paper house style now insisted the organisation were 'purveyors of serious business' and promoted 'nonsense for life'.

On the day of the fete itself I remember a sense of people eyeing each other up in an act of generational evaluation. There were elements in the atmosphere of Curtain Road and Great Eastern Road whose significance had yet to be defined.

In one's early twenties excess is so unexceptional as to seem mundane, but Joshua had always enjoyed the competitive nature of hedonism for hedonism's sake.

Although by no means from anything other than a well-to-do west London background, Joshua lacked a private income and the deeper his immersion in the art world, the more he increasingly realised that however entertaining his ideas, manifestos and broadsides or however accomplished his organisational skill, without supplementary finance he was destined to experience the same penury as any artist living by their wits.

Joshua continued to polish his boots and shoes with aggression and his clothes still reflected his idiosyncratic style, but his appearance, even when bedecked in tweeds, sometimes gave the impression that the basic amenities at Factual Nonsense were inadequate. There was no shortage of flats, studios or houses he could visit for ablutions or home-cooked food, but he increasingly had the air of someone who was not taking enough care of themselves. A rash intermittently covered his neck and, however well tailored his second-hand clothes may have once been, they were often creased with the lacklustre dowdiness of unlaundered fabric that had been slept in too many times. Letters from bailiffs and auditors were an increasingly common occurrence and there were various creditors occupying his time, and the folds across his forehead offset the etiolated pallor of his complexion. As with anyone with such reckless self-belief and energy, there was a dark side to his moods; the thin pink scars on his forearms that had been an intermittent feature of his teenage years occasionally reappeared.

I wondered, for all his self-promotional flair, if he had begun to tire of the art world.

In an interview filmed on the roof of Factual Nonsense Joshua described his ambitions for himself and the gallery:

> I'm much more interested in the aesthetisisation of daily life than I am in the guarding of so called critical high standards within the arts establishment itself

Sounding ponderous and at his most patrician, he goes on to suggest that he will have succeeded when there is:

> better housing, better factories, better landscape, better Woolworths.

Joshua was beginning to witness the gradual commodification of his ideas and of the work he had exhibited in particular, a process that habitually sees the unorthodox absorbed into the establishment, an establishment that Joshua himself had been keen to invite to the Courtauld Institute and into his gallery.

The energy and commitment he had dedicated to maintaining his presence in the nascent East London artistic community had, along with the initial financial patronage he had secured, started to diminish. As he became aware of subtle shifts in philanthropy developing around him and witnessed the change in perception of the area, Joshua doubtless felt a similar reversal in his own momentum.

*

During the phone call I had received in Revolver informing me of his death I learned that there was speculation as to whether he had taken his own life or if, late one night at Factual Nonsense, there had been an unintentional moment of tragedy. Joshua had been discovered on the platform bed within easy reach of which had stood a bottle of laudanum; I had initially been told, presumably along with most of those who had been contacted, that a handkerchief drenched in ether had also been found. It was later reported that the bottle of laudanum had belonged to an antique medicine cabinet and had had a cracked seal. Whatever the exact formulation of the opiate or its provenance, Joshua had begun inhaling its vapours in order to sleep. This bed-time ritual was a fairly recent development and one he usually undertook while drunk.

Whether or not he was conscious of his final actions Joshua had tragically underestimated both his tolerance for alcohol and the strain he had placed on himself as a figurehead for other people's work.

Throughout his life Joshua had talked about death with such a frequency that conversations on the subject could quickly turn banal. My shock at learning of his death was accompanied by an unbearable sense of despair.

At a gallery opening a year or so later I saw footage of myself crying at Joshua's wake. It formed part of a video installation by Dan Asher, an artist who had exhibited at Factual Nonsense. I was extremely angry when I first saw the work but my emotions steadied and I wondered whether it was the kind of distraught juxtaposition of which Joshua would have approved.

As I arrived at Revolver I searched through piles of junk hoping to locate the cassette copy of *Every Picture Tells a Story* that I was convinced would reveal itself and had become emblematic of something I had yet to understand.

After twenty minutes of upturning boxes and restructuring piles of faded paperwork that I had pulled to pieces only to disassemble again, I accepted that the tape was lost.

I retrieved a vinyl copy of the album from the second-hand section and attempted to listen to the record, prepared as I was to be reduced to tears once more.

Within a few minutes I heard the involuntarily 'Hey!' in the title track that Joshua and I had discovered and yelped along to in France. The hours I had spent on the Revolver stool discovering similar accidents and anomalies in records – a throat being cleared at the start of the Wailing

Souls *Firehouse Rock*, the vigorous coughing fit during 'TV Eye' on the Stooges *Fun House* – had all been prompted by closely listening to *Every Picture Tells a Story* years before.

The significance of detecting spontaneous outbursts such as these suddenly and forcefully struck me as trivial. For the first time I felt that Revolver, the days and years I had passed there and the habits the shop had helped me develop, might be inconsequential, perhaps even witless.

I was aware that music's power to heal and console was one of its primary functions. I had similarly often read about its capacity for saving people's lives, but such notions were currently beyond my recognition. The death of a close friend – one whose funeral was attended and in part organised by a generation of artists that would be distinguished by their ability to win prizes and feted as arbiters of a new, fractious, moneyed culture – left me unresponsive.

I sat on the stool and realised that listening to Rod Stewart would offer me no solace or redemption and I wept, and then wept again.

9

I always enjoyed working on Saturdays. There was usually a period during the day when custom was brisk and records and cash changed hands with a momentum that stimulated the shop's atmosphere. For these few hours neither was it necessary to dwell on the purpose or nature of Revolver, nor was there time to comment on customers' purchases. However enjoyable this wellspring of adrenaline, it was never sufficient to dispel the ensuing torpor at the start of the following week.

If a band of reasonable stature, particularly a touring American act, was playing in Bristol on a Saturday night, the shop would fill with a clientele drawn from their audience. These new and temporary customers travelled to the city from towns that lacked independent record shops and bought stock that had stubbornly remained unhandled in the racks.

There was another type of casual customer who restricted their experience of Revolver to Saturdays. These were professional couples on a morning or afternoon shopping trip to Park Street and Queens Road who entered the shop with discernible trepidation. Their clothes were tailored and they usually carried shopping bags bearing the logo of the boutiques and kitchenware shops nearby. Once inside, the male half of the couple would approach the counter after a furtive glance at the new release section. The female half would remain near the window. Both might linger at the erratic and unconvincing CD section arranged in a manner that demonstrated in what little regard the format was held in the shop.

It was hard not to sense the awkwardness of members of the public who had entered the shop for the first time and with a specific request.

There was an infantile and unpleasant pleasure to be had at witnessing such moments of tension. The staff had grown so accustomed to the atmosphere in Revolver that the sense of intimidation it could convey in the lay music buyer was easily overlooked. The shop had in some ways magnificently resisted embracing CDs even when their sales achieved substantial profit margins. Instead, Revolver was a shop specialising in vinyl at a moment when vinyl was dying.

There would be an occasion on most Saturdays when the number of new visitors drawn from passing trade displaced our core clientele and the shop underwent a subtle shift in energy, as though it had temporarily been taken out of our hands into new ownership. Roger was keen not to appear offensive to anyone unfamiliar and, in perhaps the only instance of staff training, urged us to be polite to hesitant and wary potential customers.

I had noticed a change in behaviour of these professional, career-minded shoppers. They arrived at the counter with the name of an artist and album title written on a note and asked specifically for that record and indicated that they wished to purchase it on CD. I was often struck by the relative obscurity of the title they were searching for and the genre of music to which I presumed it belong. Equally, I was arrogant enough to be surprised at the customer's lack of desire to buy anything other than their chosen album. In what I considered an atypical request two years earlier, a local man who worked a few doors down the road from Revolver and whom I knew to be a lettings agent, asked for the new album by the Malian singer Oumou Sangare. The release had never been stocked, nor was likely to be, but I was impressed by the sense of adventure in the enquiry. A year later one half of a professional couple walked confidently to the counter and asked for 'the new Justin Vali Trio CD', a name that was wholly unfamiliar to Roger and myself.

'Justin Vali, what sort of music is that? Roger enquired.

'He's from Madagascar,' the customer replied. 'Violin player, great music.'

'Madagascar!' said Roger 'We have a world music section,' he went on, as he pointed towards several dividers full of vinyl. 'Never heard of Ju-s-tin V-a-l-i though.'

'Thanks,' said the customer, who promptly turned and left the shop.

'Madagascar!' Roger said again, his tone pitched between bewilderment and despair.

The indigenous music of the global south classified and marketed under the laboured phrase 'world music' had a large audience in Bristol. In the early 1980s *The Bristol Recorder*, a periodical in the form of a vinyl album, ran to three issues. The second issue included three songs by Peter Gabriel at whose suggestion the third and final *Bristol Recorder* featured the Ghanaian group Ekomé.

Out of this affiliation between the founders of *The Bristol Recorder* and Gabriel grew the WOMAD festival and record label, whose releases were distributed, as had been *The Bristol Recorder*, by Revolver.

At the time the shop embraced the interest in world music itself and released a record by the highlife band Ivory Coasters on its Recreational Records label in 1982. There was a degree of militancy about the record. One of its three tracks was titled 'The Bongo That Ate Pik Botha' and on the poster produced to advertise the release were included images of colonial rule and native insurgency. Underneath the pictures a short unattributed paragraph of text increased this sense of militancy:

No ordinary band these, but fearless and daring. With eyes that flashed and glinted as savagely as the eyes of their mounts; especially one, whose long, slender spear-head was pointing straight at Tiger's breast. The arm that held the spear was bent backwards, it had only to move forward and the spear head would dart towards the white man's chest like a serpent's tongue!

In certain areas of the city, where the currents of 1980s activism remained strong, it was possible to detect an enduring affection for the perceived glamour of Third World revolutions. When I first lived in Bristol, the embrace of certain identities that later became known as alternative lifestyle choices was easily discernible. A shop on the waterfront was one of several that specialised in goods imported from the Caucasus. It was alone in stocking millinery imported from Afghanistan where the nine-year war with Soviet Russia was drawing to an end. The shop sold ephemera from the conflict including ammunition boxes and both the ushanka fur hats worn by the Soviet military and the soft wool pakuls worn by the Mujahideen rebels.

The rolled-up pakuls became fashionable in the streets where identity politics flourished and were worn as if in solidarity with the Mujahideen. A friend of mine studying the history of Central Asia found their popularity perplexing. In an attempt to point out what he considered the absurdity of their being taken up by those who supported progressive causes, he would occasionally raise his fist in a gesture of solidarity and exclaim, 'No Education For Women!' when passing anyone whose head sported a pakul.

World music concerts were popular in Bristol but Revolver would rarely received visits from members of the community that comprised their audience. The African section remained well stocked, but with records that had been placed in its dividers several years earlier. I was at a loss to explain the sudden interest in Malian and Congolese musicians, particularly from the professional rather than bohemian classes. A month later I began to understand the music's renewed popularity and change in audience. A harried-looking man in his mid-forties walked briskly to the counter and with his finger pointing in the air, as if at a bar ordering a round of drinks, said,

'The one by the Mavericks and the one by Papa Wemba, please.'

'I'm not sure we have either of those in stock,' I replied, knowing full well we were unaware of both releases, but keen to maintain an air of civility.

'Really!' he said. 'Didn't you see them last night? Really good musicians, the Mavericks. They're just like Roy Orbison.'

At this moment Roger intervened.

'We've got some Roy Orbison LPs, some greatest hits, the songs he recorded for Monument . . . the good stuff . . .'

'No, I don't want Roy Orbison, thanks, just the Mavericks and Papa Wemba.'

'How many Roy Orbison albums have you got?' asked Roger, with a smile.

'None,' said the visitor.

'Well, buy some Roy. Don't worry about these people who sound like him, buy the original.'

The visitor had started to grow uncomfortable.

'Tha-n-ks guys,' he said with a forced laugh.

'But I want what I saw last night. I didn't come here for anything else.'

As he turned to leave the shop Roger and I exchanged glances. A regular customer who had been inspecting a box of CDs on the counter looked around to establish the shop was quiet then gestured us to approach.

'He must have seen that programme last night,' he said, his eyes wincing slightly.

'*Later*, it is,' he continued, 'with that bloke from Squeeze.'

I had lived without a television for some years and Roger watched his rarely. Neither of us was aware of this relatively new music programme, but its presence and programming decisions explained the requests the shop had received for world music and other genres that appealed to our irregular or new Saturday visitors. I accepted that it was in the shop's interest to attempt to stock these items and made enquiries with distributors to learn that many of the acts featured on the programme were sold to shops with healthy discounts and supporting marketing campaigns. Although, if Revolver were to order any copies, I was informed, the supplier would charge full price, as the shop had failed to register any previous interest and the discount period had subsequently ended.

To participate in such campaigns would have had little effect on our trade, but the fact Revolver had been ignored added to my sense that the shop was increasingly remote from the retail mainstream to which there was barely an alternative. Our lack of a chart-return machine rendered us ineligible for promotional discounts. As the shop was unable to record sales it missed the opportunities distributors offered, such as greatly reduced or even free stock, in order that their titles be registered.

The culture of selling records had undergone subtle shifts of which we were unaware, or had chosen to ignore. Many independent shops offered a set of turntables so customers could listen to records before purchase. I struggled to recall anyone asking to hear a release in Revolver as most of our customers assumed such a request would be declined.

A precedent for what anyone visiting Revolver might consider acceptable to ask of the staff had been set many years previously.

As a student I had once asked to hear *On Fire*, the latest album by Galaxie 500.

'Hear it?' Roger had said. 'Why?'

Before I managed to assert myself and explain the reasons, Roger gave a rational qualification for his surprise at my request.

'Did you like the last one?' he asked.

'Yes, I thought it . . .'

'Well, buy this one then,' Roger interrupted. 'It sounds exactly the same.'

Such exchanges had become so frequent that the majority of customers were deterred from asking again.

The distribution companies we dealt with had recently changed the day of their weekly delivery. New stock now arrived on Saturday mornings rather, as had been the convention, on the Monday of release. This decision was taken to allow shops to open their doors with that week's albums and singles ready for immediate purchase. The business of marketing had developed into a highly technical practice that required, especially according to those whose profession it was, dedicated expertise and this change in delivery days had been facilitated in order that their skill might flourish and produce sales.

In Revolver our reaction to such changes was to file the newly arrived stock on Saturday mornings and place it in the racks for immediate sale. When staff from a distributor indicated that the shop might be in breach of its terms of trade, our standard reply was to plead ignorance of the phrase and ask for an explanation.

From the distributors and record companies there was a further shift towards professionalism in their desire to coerce, then manage, contributions from record shops to promote the albums they considered a priority. On a radiant weekday morning in early September, a sales rep, excited by the thought of a busy autumn, presented us with a pre-release cassette of the new album by a band Roger, I and most of our customers, found intolerable. The tape was handed over to us with the accompanying instruction that it should be played at exactly two o'clock on the following Saturday afternoon. The rep explained that he and his colleagues would be visiting several independent retailers on the prescribed day and time and if they arrived at a shop to find it playing this pre-release cassette, the store would receive a cash prize. On receiving this information Roger, in full view of the rep, instantly gave away the cassette to an unfamiliar middle-aged man who was preoccupied by the records in the dub section.

Our continual refusal to engage with marketing and its accompanying protocol held a fleeting sense of amusement; although, rather than acts of defiance, these minor conflicts felt illustrative of Revolver's unremitting decline. For all our regular customers who visited the shop expecting to engage in badinage, there was a larger number who, having in their eyes been humiliated, decided never to return.

If Roger could appear abrasive with customers, I regarded the liveliness of these interactions as an essential facet of his energy and enthusiasm for music. More than once I witnessed him talk a customer out of completing the purchase of the record they had brought to the counter. Instead Roger would suggest they spent their money on a different, often cheaper, record.

These instances of magnanimity could backfire. A somewhat shy, quietly spoken customer once stood at the counter with a record by the James Taylor Quartet.

'I can't sell you that,' said Roger. 'All that record is, is a complete rip off of *The Cat* by Jimmy Smith. Buy *The Cat* instead it's over there, in the jazz section.'

With colour rising in her cheeks the customer attempted to locate *The Cat* while drawing as little attention to herself as possible, only to be loudly reprimanded by Roger for looking in the J rather than the S divider in the jazz section. Her final visit to Revolver concluded with an attempt to look as inconspicuous as possible while walking briskly towards the door.

Roger's reasons for declining custom were occasionally less altruistic. If he saw bags containing purchases from rival record shops brought into Revolver, he would, depending on his mood, either ask the owner to leave or advise them that they had been placed on a final warning not to bring such bags in again.

I had grown accustomed to opening the back door to acquaintances of Roger bearing large cans of olive oil or similar items. After a brief exchange of pleasantries and goods they would depart with a bag of vinyl. These acts of barter held a charm that contributed to a sense of buoyancy, one that the shop, now so adrift from orthodoxy, needed in order to survive. On completion of the transactions, once the farewells had been made, the departures of these customers left us to ponder the shop's impecunious state and the reality that our distributors and suppliers had placed their accounts on hold.

The difficulties and the rhythm of our cash flow was so familiar that I assumed every shop suffered equivalent financial hardships. Every year Revolver sold hundreds of tickets priced at £40 or £50 for Glastonbury Festival. In April, May and June these sales helped maintain the shop's accounts, although the festival often received payment only several months later.

One Christmas I had grown so used to answering calls from the festival that I presumed every time the phone rang that Jean from the Glastonbury office, the wife of Michael Eavis, was on the other end of the receiver demanding settlement. The calls were made with such regularity that I began answering the phone with 'Hello, Jean'. To which she would reply, 'Is he there?'

When I replied that Roger had left for the day, Jean asked after his health, the viability of the shop and urged me to ask Roger to make payment whenever he could. She also indicated that Revolver were the last of the festival's outlets to make payment and would be unlikely to be able to sell tickets the following year. There were never threats, however, of litigation or reprisal and their generosity and patience was rewarded when Roger managed to settle the outstanding liability within a few months.

As customers arrived, looked through the racks then

slowly left, their empty-handed departure gave the impression they had long grown tired of seeing the same wilting sleeves at the front of each divider. This feeling of having nothing to offer, of being so lacklustre, was new. Friends and regular visitors would walk to the counter for conversation alone, all too aware that there was little likelihood of the shop stocking any recent record they had heard or read about, and were too polite to enquire of its availability.

On certain days I was convinced I had listened to every record in Revolver, those on display and those hidden from view. After a desolate three hours during which I had been entirely alone I glanced at the different formats – tapes, CDs, 10"s, 7"s, 12"s, LPs and bootleg recordings of every genre – that surrounded me. I suddenly found their presence haunting rather than stimulating. My familiarity with every sleeve and surface and the thin film of dust that shrouded and dulled their artwork felt irrational and purposeless. I grew nauseous at the thought of listening to any of the music contained within their covers. I was aware that Roger experienced similar feelings. I would occasionally leave him alone in the shop during the late afternoon listening to Radio 4.

However, there remained riches to be heard in Revolver, although I frequently had to summon the will to experience them. As I put the phone down following another call chasing payment, I lingered in front of a pile of cassettes stacked on the shelf facing me. The tapes largely consisted of concerts performed in Bristol in recent years that had been taped by our friends or periodically by the sound men of a venue who, knowing our interest in an act that had played there, had generously provided us with a copy at the end of the performance.

My eyes settled on one cassette in particular. It was a recording of a Townes Van Zandt concert that had taken place at the Fleece & Firkin in the spring of 1994. For the period I worked in the shop, records by Van Zandt had always been difficult to obtain. His catalogue was scarcely in stock with distributors and then only available as imports priced at a premium.

In particular the albums he recorded in the 1970s for the Poppy label, an independent record company in New York that was now bankrupt, were rarely available. Occasionally a wholesaler might include Van Zandt titles on their inventory, and shop-soiled copies arrived in cut-out sleeves as imports from Germany where the songwriter had a notable following and performed regularly.

In a desultory mood I played the cassette of the Fleece concert. The recording was of poor quality and the presence of hiss on the tape compounded, on first listening at least, the sense of distance and detachment inherent in the performance. Van Zandt gave long, sometimes incoherent introductions to his most familiar songs such as 'Pancho and Lefty', 'Tecumseh Valley' and 'Waiting Around to Die'.

The harsh sound of glasses being placed and stacked on the venue's long bar could often be heard during these passages.

Van Zandt was audibly frail between numbers, although his voice was strong and sounded wounded and brave and inhabited by a spirit that was hard to control. The regularity with which he had given concerts over the preceding twenty years ensured his voice had little trouble reaching the notes, or conveying their melodiousness. Even if he was singing the songs by rote, the bleakness that was his alone could be heard as he performed them seated on the Fleece & Firkin's sparse stage.

He sang a verse from 'She Came and She Touched Me' with a tenderness that articulated the poignancy of the lyric and of his situation, repeating himself with the same songs every night:

> The moments do somersaults
> Into eternity,
> Cling to their coat tails
> And beg them to stay.

When he toured Germany Van Zandt played venues larger than the Fleece & Firkin. They were usually run by a town or community organisation and subsidised by the local authority or their equivalent of the Arts Council. As part of the arrangement for the concerts, performers were offered accommodation, a practice common in mainland Europe but rare in the UK. Although the accommodation provided was often little more than a basic hotel, to visit Germany for a month was consequently an attractive and viable proposition for many acts, particularly American artists who could attract a higher ticket price.

The tape from the Fleece & Firkin was nearing the end of the concert as Van Zandt started 'For the Sake of the Song':

Maybe she just has to sing for the sake of the song,
Who do I think that I am to decide that she's wrong?

I had heard stories that Van Zandt was a difficult person to manage, that he had regular and perilous experiences with alcohol and drugs and that once, having been urged at breakfast to eat, he asked for an extra slice of celery with his morning Bloody Mary.

I pictured his life spent on tour in Germany, sleeping in modest hotels with worn linen where his overnight stay was subsidised by the local authority. It was widely understood that Revolver never specialised in any given genre, but the thought struck me that perhaps our expertise lay in championing the music I was currently listening to, the genre played by musicians who stayed in decrepit hotels, for the sake of the song.

Perhaps, I thought while seated on a stool listening to a bootleg tape, Revolver had finally become their record-shop equivalent. At that moment the sullenness I was experiencing waned and was replaced instead with a more powerful feeling, one similar to the experience of heartbreak, as I accepted that, other than to a handful of people including myself, Revolver had become a closed ward.

As the flow of customers searching for releases the shop was unable or unwilling to stock increased, I reflected on why Revolver had grown so abject and adrift. In our different manners each member of staff was reasonably effective at selling music. Roger, in particular, could convince a stranger to buy any record to which he attached strong emotions. Visitors to the shop from outside Bristol would return months later, enriched by the experience of buying music that, before conversing with Roger, they had previously been unaware of.

They treasured the atmosphere of enquiry and compulsion at the counter, even if it felt intimidating, and departed smiling and enlivened, carrying their purchases in the red-and-black Revolver bag, sure that in doing so some mutually appreciated form of status had been conferred. In turn they brought their particular enthusiasms to the counter for discussion and used the opportunity of loitering in the shop to broaden their musical knowledge.

Revolver allowed an access to the past that was rare. It placed emphasis on the canon it curated and attempted to stock, and was sceptical about new records and the frenetic manner in which many were mediated and released. If an album was out of print or unavailable, a trustworthy customer might gain access to a copy from Roger's private collection or from the back-room shelves. The records in the shop were merely a display that served as an introduction to a larger and deeper archive, one that could be reached only with Roger's assessment and approval of whoever had pleaded to hear the rare, inviolable vinyl stored there. The process by which Roger decided who was allowed access to this archive escaped me.

Customers, for whom the experience of the shop was rich and extended beyond the transaction of buying records, had acquired the Revolver canon. For these records that the shop habitually lionised and venerated there was little further demand in the city. Underneath the shop turntable was a row of twenty-five copies of *Pagan Strings* by Blurt, a band dear to Roger's heart. Blurt, whose music blended tone poetry, saxophone and paranoid rhythms, had started in the early 1980s and followed a self-determined trajectory of modest popularity. Roger first met the band in Cheltenham and remained a supporter throughout their career, with an agitated enthusiasm that echoed their music.

The copies of *Pagan Strings* stored near the counter were supplied directly by the band and had sold in their dozens over the previous two to three years. The music did not conform to the currents of the mid-1990s and could only be enjoyed on its own terms. The record received no press or airplay, but Roger had attested to its strengths and sold these copies out of enthusiasm alone. Revolver may have sold as many as 150 copies of *Pagan Strings* all told. Our core customers, those who enjoyed the challenge of listening to our recommendations, but no one else, had bought *Pagan Strings*. The remaining twenty-five copies served to remind us that the reach of the music championed by the shop was slender. Although the thought remained unarticulated, I was aware other record stores sold unnervingly large numbers of CDs to customers who considered Revolver volatile and eccentric.

It had become a habit of ours to expatiate on the limited interest in the records that remained on the shelves as an example of the poverty of imagination in the average music fan and their susceptibility to distracting and meaningless musical trends. Now there was a creeping realisation that the poverty was not just that of our credit lines with distributors, but ours.

For the preceding three years I had listened to the records stored in the back room and absorbed the stories and secrets they contained. It occurred to me that these experiences might also have made me grow listless and complacent.

I thought of the anecdotes that were now staples in pub conversations about Revolver, such as how Roger had assembled a new area of shelving behind the till, only to tap his handiwork with pride at the very moment these new units started to subside and slowly collapse, distributing their contents onto the carpet. In a more subdued instance of physical theatre, a customer wishing to use a credit card had had the plastic returned to him in two pieces, as Roger had accidently bent the card in half while explaining that the shop did not accept payment in that form.

Revolver had as uneasy a relationship with in-store promotion as it did with any form of payment other than cash or cheque. This was typified by the experience of the comedian and performer Frank Sidebottom, who had once participated in an unsuccessful record-signing in the shop. Sidebottom was permanently in character, a condition that required him to wear a large, circular papier-mâché head at all times. A misunderstanding had occurred concerning the scheduling for the event, so when Frank Sidebottom made his public appearance in Revolver the shop was bereft of customers and staff, other than Roger.

In what doubtless felt like a moment of great ignominy for both parties, Sidebottom and Roger held a strained and muted half-hour conversation in an empty shop. As Sidebottom leant on the counter, Roger stood as far back from its surface as possible, arms folded, and made the minimum level of eye contact required to maintain discourse with Sidebottom's spheroidal head.

Such stories were now well rehearsed and often provoked laughter in their telling, during which I always felt as though I were championing Roger and our commitment to the non-conformist nature and inexpressible ethos of Revolver. For the first time I was now conscious of their pathos and that the atmosphere in which I was spending my days might have institutionalised me.

Each morning, aware that the shop was likely to be empty and deliveries rare, I had taken to playing the same, side-long track of a record taken from the back room. In the rare moments that the shop had visitors, I was habitually asked about the record as it played through the shop stereo, but no longer felt the need to apologise for listening to an album unavailable for purchase.

The piece of music was 'Boat-Woman-Song' from *Canaxis* 5, a collaboration of electronic compositions between Holger Czukay, the bassist and recordings editor of Can, and Rolf Dammers, a fellow experimental musician. 'Boat-Woman-Song' was created in 1968 from loops made of a *rondet de carole* by the thirteenth-century French composer Adam de la Halle, and of the eldritch cry of a Vietnamese woman singing a traditional song. These two elements are manipulated into a drone, over which further recordings of voices singing in an unearthly register are added and mutated to produce a sedative if eerie tonal composition.

Part of the recording was composed at the Studio for Electronic Music in Köln, the studio regularly used by Karlheinz Stockhausen under whom Czukay had been a pupil immediately prior to the creation of Canaxis 5. The influence of Stockhausen, particularly the idea of 'transformation' that the composer utilised in his 'Kurzwellen' from the previous year, in which he adapted radio signals into musical form can be heard in 'Boat-Woman-Song', as can the manipulation of voices on 'Gesang der Jünglinge' from a decade earlier.

The source tapes used on 'Boat-Woman-Song' are gradually overlapped and distorted until a sense of disintegrating and unsettled flow envelops the recording and the listener is submerged in its current.

It was possible to hear the piece as a meditative collage of esoteric and processed loops. I listened to 'Boat-Woman-Song' with such regularity that in its fractured electrical swell I was experiencing catharsis, and in my more despondent moods I recognised that Revolver was being carried downstream by its undertow, towards an inevitable fate.

As yet another customer departed from the counter empty-handed, I admitted to myself that Revolver had unintentionally started a long, harrowing closing-down sale. Rather than merely ceasing to trade, this winding-up process would represent a closure of the soul.

Revolver finally shut its doors a few months into the twenty-first century. In my heart I knew Roger found these years difficult and that the financial pressures that had been brought to bear were hard to tolerate.

Outwardly he remained self-assured and rarely articulated his emotions, although I had once asked Roger if he intended carry on with Revolver.

'What else is there?' he said. 'What greater pleasure than this?'

In an often-empty shop, I had been given an education from someone whose knowledge and love of music ran to a depth I would rarely again encounter in a life spent working in the music business. The joy I shared at listening to a record in his company was irreplaceable, as was the energy with which he heard and loved music.

The end was protracted and painful. In the last eighteen months of Revolver's existence students and casual visitors would walk through the door asking for details of the discounts on offer. Roger, having never seen them before, would curse them.

On 3 December 1996 I spent my last day in Revolver. As he brought the A-board into the corridor from under the black winter night of the pavement, I handed Roger my keys.

That evening I had considered joining friends of mine who were attending a Townes Van Zandt concert at the Borderline in London but our plans fell through. As he stumbled through his songs, his mind and voice distorted by a year spent on the road, the performance was frequently incomprehensible and was to be his last.

10

On an autumn morning in October 2013, before the clocks were put back, I walked up the wide pavements of Park Street in sunlight so strong I felt it keenly through my sweater.

The tone of the sky was of such brilliance that most of the customers in the cafés at the top of its hill were seated outside wearing sunglasses which, together with their gilets and down jackets and the steepness of Park Street, created the momentary impression of a ski resort.

As I began my journey that morning, the reasons for my visit had been clear to me. Now, as I absorbed the energy around me and re-familiarised myself with the pace of Bristol, I was reminded of the title of a song from a record I first heard in Revolver, 'Non-Cognitive Aspects of the City' by the saxophonist Joseph Jarman, a member of the Art Ensemble of Chicago. It was taken from the album *Song For* released in 1968. The song was fourteen minutes long and featured Jarman reciting a prose poem over scattered accompaniment.

One evening after we had shut the shop Roger introduced me to the record and the work of the Art Ensemble. As well as explaining that the members of the Ensemble contributed to each other's solo recordings, Roger discussed the meaning of the acronym A.A.C.M. (The Association for the Advancement of Creative Musicians), an organisation the ensemble had helped found in 1965 and whose initials were written on many of their releases.

'If you see those letters on the back of a record, it'll be worth hearing,' he said.

'Non-cognitive Aspects of the City.'

As I walked through Clifton in the sunshine, I found myself repeating the title of Jarman's prose poem and out of the depths of memory, one of the lines spoken in his soft but purposeful voice came to me:

> Non-cognitive these elements of how
> No more

An echo of the elegiac tone in which he had delivered the last two words was carried on the soothing breeze that welcomed me as I reached the Triangle and saw, in the middle distance, the building that had once been home to Revolver.

I had decided to write about the shop a few months earlier and was reconciled to the idea that in order to capture the spirit of Revolver, it was necessary for me to stand in its rooms once more, to be reminded of its physical as well as emotional space and to push and pull the handles of the door that had opened and closed across its threshold.

Although I trusted my memories I was not prepared for the overwhelming emotions they prompted. If I could gain access to the building, take photographs and measurements, be sure of its dimensions and stand once more under the ceiling, I would at least be able to corroborate my thoughts and recollections with facts.

As I drew nearer and saw its site more clearly, I began to suspect my motivation for writing about Revolver and for revisiting its location. These were streets and locations from another life, one that was better left undisturbed.

My friends in the city had grown accustomed to seeing a hand-written sign fixed to what had been the shop entrance, 'Exciting Retail Opportunity, 1,500 sq. ft', accompanied by a mobile phone number. The sign had been in place for more than a decade. Since the day Roger had loaded his van with the final consignment of boxes of unsold stock and vacated the premises, Revolver, or rather the network of rooms that had been its home for thirty years had lain empty.

Some weeks earlier I had successfully searched for an image of the sign affixed to the doorway online and made a note of the phone number. As I looked at the still photograph of the building on my computer screen I was surprised by the effect it had on my senses. The exterior had been painted a peculiar grey colour and the windows that ran the length of the corridor had recently been cleaned. Rather than making the former site of Revolver look an attractive proposition, these basic attempts at gentrification had left the premises looking lack-lustre and partially explained why they remained unoccupied.

The emotional drag I experienced while concentrating on these details strengthened. In that instant I decided to ring the number written on the sign and to make contact with the past in order to begin a process that might lead to resolution.

The phone rang for the length that usually signifies that the call will be answered by an instruction to leave a message. To my surprise a hoarse voice began shouting at the other end:

''Alloh!'

'Hello, is that Ivor?

''Alloh'

'Ivor?'

'Bahh, its no good.'

'Ivor, are you in Berkeley Crescent?'

'Ah? Yes! Who are you?'

'Ivor! Thank you! I will try you again!'

In that short and fractured conversation I established that the number belonged to Ivor, who had once been Revolver's landlord and evidently still owned the building. He had always been hard of hearing, a condition that had clearly deteriorated in the intervening years.

Now that I had confirmation that Ivor still lived in the upper floors of the building, I was sure that if I travelled to Bristol and knocked loudly on his door, explained the reasons for my visit and perhaps offered him a small cash payment, he would grant me access to what had once been Revolver.

At Berkeley Crescent I crossed the road and made my way towards the steps that led to Ivor's door. As I was about to mount the stairwell I immediately came to a sudden halt. To my right a door, the former entrance to Revolver, was ajar. In the following thirty seconds disbelief, excitement and fear competed together for my reason. Without hesitation I pushed at the door to open it further. Before I had had time to consider my actions, I found myself staring along the corridor, utterly unprepared for the disorientation that followed.

I felt I had been thrust the length of the corridor at terrifying speed while long-buried fragments of memory surfaced from my subconscious. Conversations, flashes of red-and-black Revolver bags, coats, hair, arguments, laughter, sweat, smiles, raised voices and frequencies from the shop sound system flooded my senses. When I had taken the decision to write about this place, I had attempted as careful an evaluation as possible of how prepared I was to dispel and contain the nostalgia such an undertaking was certain to provoke. The emotions I experienced in those long minutes as I stared, stricken, down the corridor were altogether more disorientatingly powerful.

I drew breath and, in an attempt to come to terms with how overwhelmed I felt and in a reaction that frightened me with its instinct, held on to the railing that still ran along the corridor. The sensation of a physical object, even one so loaded with memory, helped me regain my composure and I began to come to terms with the desolate and haunted environment I had entered.

The shop door, windows and width of the corridor all seemed to be of differing proportions from those I remembered. The surfaces and surrounding walls had been whitewashed haphazardly in a rushed manner, creating the impression that it had been Ivor's wish to erase the memory of Revolver.

The paint that had been used was cheap and barely an undercoat deep, and the sense that history had been only partially concealed added to the resonance of what this lifeless space once represented.

The sight of an open door and unfamiliar staircase interrupted the absorption in my surroundings. I heard footsteps shuffle in the distance and, aware of his hearing difficulties began calling Ivor's name. Initially Ivor was wary of my presence. He asked a number of questions and relaxed when I was able to answer them with anecdotes of my time in the shop. More than once he asked if I was a reporter but grew contented as I began to mention Roger's name with regularity.

'Oh, Roger,' he said smiling. 'They told me not to touch him with a bargepole, they did, the people who had the shop before him. The rent was never on time.'

'There hasn't been anyone in here since, has there?' I asked.

'No, we painted it and got rid of all the rubbish. An art gallery or a wine bar you see, that's what I thought. Or a bike shop, that's popular here now, bikes, but you couldn't get the bikes up the stairs so easily could you? You see.'

Ivor said he now recognised me, although, as the conversation developed, I was aware that he was frailer then I had noticed, in both body and mind. I grew aware of time once more and asked if he might kindly allow me to spend some minutes in what had been the shop and back room.

The nervousness and bewilderment I experienced a few minutes earlier had subsided. As I stood in the room that had once been home to such an infinite number of records and record sleeves, I gave an involuntarily sigh of happiness. I walked towards the counter that was still in position, as was the uncharacteristically elegant light fitting that had illuminated our conversation and desires.

I made my way back into the corridor in order to gain access to the back room. Ivor had remained standing near its door and struck up conversation again.

'Roger. Let me see. Were you here when he called the fire brigade? Oh dear me! The water was coming down from the roof you see. It was the middle of summer. I was up there with a woman. I'd left the bath running and I wouldn't answer the door, I didn't want the fire engine to see me, you see. I saw the flashing blue lights, the firemen were knocking on the door but I was in there with a woman.'

'Roger,' he smiled. 'I had mates in Cheltenham. Did you ever meet them? They told me not to touch him with a bargepole. He was here the longest out of all of them I suppose.'

I loitered near Ivor as he spoke. I was conscious that my unexpected visit had perhaps set in motion memories he too had thought had gone and that by prompting him to dwell on Roger, the perpetually late rent payments, their arguments and animosity, I had unwittingly forced Ivor to reflect on the emptiness of the premises for so many years and the unlikeliness of their being used again.

Ivor bade me enter the back room and remained in the corridor. The shelves that once groaned with vinyl had all been removed. It was now possible to see all four corners unhindered by boxes, tables and debris. I felt the slightest presence of some unknown and unknowable anima beside me, in this room that had once felt so clandestine and intoxicating.

I glanced over my shoulder to see Ivor lost in thought and smiling while staring at his feet. Although I realised that it would not be possible to rouse him from this reverie, I gestured that I would proceed further into the room, towards the counter.

The interior of the building had been whitewashed like the outside. A window in the back room against which boxes had always been stacked now illuminated the walls. As I stepped behind the counter this sense of light and radiance contributed to my giddiness. The same wooden units, constructed over the years by the shop's various owners, surrounded me. Underneath the counter were shelves purpose built for housing vinyl. For the last thirteen years they had stored only dust.

I placed my fingertips on the counter then pressed with my palms in order to feel its resilience. The unpredictable and unresolved emotions I had felt on first entering the shop subsided when I began my conversation with Ivor. As I looked out from the counter I felt only love; love for the people who had stood here, under these lights, love for anyone whose lives were enriched by the music they bought under this roof and love, an unquantifiable love, for the rows of records that had sat before me offering the richest of lives, one both dominated and enraptured by music, the healing force of the universe, the food of love.

The surface of the counter had grown warm under my hands. From a recess in my mind that this journey to Revolver had unlocked I heard the opening chords of a song, 'The Spirit World Rising' by Daniel Johnston, which I had played incessantly within these four walls so many years before. At that moment I felt that the spirit world had risen in a ghost dance and we were moving together, in time.